Have Dog Will Travel

Oregon Edition

Barbara Whitaker

Ginger & Spike Publications

May all your Travels be wonderful!
Barb Whitaker
—and Ginger

Printed in the United States of America

Second printing, February 1999

Publisher's Cataloging-in-Publication
(Provided by Quality Books, Inc)

Whitaker, Barbara Lee.
    Have dog will travel. Oregon edition / Barbara Whitaker. — 1st ed.
    p. cm.
    Includes bibliographical references and index.
    ISBN: 0-9660544-3-1

    1. Pets and travel—Oregon—Directories. 2. Motels—Pet accommodations—Oregon—Directories. 3. Hotels—Pet accommodations—Oregon—Directories. 4. Veterinary services—Oregon—Directories. I. Title.

SF415.45.W45 1997   647.94'795
                          QBI97-41244

Cover and interior illustrations by Bob Sleeper

Ginger & Spike Publications
PO Box 937
Wilsonville, OR 97070-0937
503/625-3001

In loving memory of
Brujo, Jack, Kala, Jeremiah,
Kaka, Irish and Almond—
faithful companions, all.

Acknowledgments

I want to thank all the wonderful folks who helped bring this book to completion—

First of all, my love and appreciation to my husband Linn, who handled our household's everyday reality with virtually never-ending patience, while I handled the book!

Thanks also to Kate Gerity—friend, advisor and editor par excellence. And to editors Susie and Bill Osborn of Susie's Country Inn; Dr. Ann Horne, Sharon Anton and Patty Doxtater—all from the Tualatin Animal Clinic; also Sherry Allmaras, Wendy Bridgewater, Shauna Gonzales and Jo Hibbits. Your suggestions and careful reading of the manuscript were much appreciated.

Kudos to Bob Sleeper for the wonderful illustrations, and to Kohel Haver and Dick Mort for their excellent legal and technical advice, respectively.

And of course, thanks to Ginger and Spike—without their daily supervision, this book would not have come into being. Way to go, guys!

Contents

Part I

Help your dog become a well-behaved traveler

Part I
Help your dog
become a
well-behaved traveler

1: Touring With Your Well-behaved Traveler

So you plan to travel around Oregon by car, and you want to take your dog along? Well, you're in good company—lots of dogs travel with their owners. My German Shepherd Ginger certainly does. After all, she's part of the family, and a vacation just wouldn't be the same without her.

Traveling with a well-behaved dog can be great fun and a minimum of fuss. But it does involve some advance planning and effort on your part. It also requires extra consideration for your fellow travelers and for the friendly people who provide your accommodations.

Part I of this book shows how you can help your dog become a well-behaved traveler—making your trips more fun for both of you.

In Part II you'll find the reference sections:

🐕 More than 700 Oregon hotels, motels, and bed & breakfast inns that welcome you and your dog, listed alphabetically by city name

🐕 Emergency veterinary clinics across the state, just in case your pet needs emergency care during your trip

🐕 Recommended training and dog care books

🐕 2-part index for locating specific information— listed alphabetically by business name or topic

How to have fun— and get invited back

The numbers of hotels, motels, and bed & breakfast inns that accept pets have been dwindling in recent years. This unfortunate trend is largely due to a small minority of dog owners who have allowed their dogs to run amok. These are the dogs who damage furnishings and landscaping, or behave aggressively toward other guests and their pets.

As responsible dog owners, we can all help to reverse this trend. Preparing in advance and taking appropriate equipment along not only ensures more enjoyable trips for ourselves and our dogs, but also provides positive examples for encouraging more establishments to accept pets.

To prepare for a great trip with your dog, you should:

🐾 Attend obedience training classes with your dog *before* you travel. Once you are both familiar with the basic commands for good behavior, you'll be ready when the unexpected happens. (And believe me, it *does* eventually happen!)

🐾 Pack the appropriate pet travel supplies

🐾 Make advance room reservations, stating clearly that you will be bringing your dog

🐾 Prepare a doggy first aid kit—and learn what to do in an emergency *before* taking your dog to the veterinary clinic

🐾 Always be aware of your dog's impact on other guests and on the facilities, both indoor and outdoor, where you're staying

These topics and more are discussed in the chapters that follow.

When to bring your dog— and when **NOT** to

Obviously you want your dog to travel with you, or you wouldn't be reading this book. But also ask yourself whether or not he *wants* to come along.

Your dog will probably enjoy the trip if:

🐕 You're traveling by car

🐕 Driving time will be fairly short, so he won't be spending long hours in the car

🐕 You've planned lots of activities that your dog can share, like hiking or walking on the beach

But consider traveling *without* your dog when:

🐕 Adverse weather conditions would make him miserably hot or cold

🐕 You're traveling by plane or train—these are more of an ordeal for your pet than a vacation

🐕 Most of your time will be spent in activities that your dog cannot share—after all, would *you* want to spend your entire vacation locked in an empty car or motel room?

And now a word from Spike

The feline member of our family ("He Who Must Be Obeyed") wants to point out that he definitely prefers to stay home while Ginger goes traveling. Call him a homebody if you like, but Spike insists that cats as a rule would much rather stay behind in their own familiar places. On Spike's advice, then, this book addresses the issues related to traveling with dogs, but not cats.

Obviously you'll be making arrangements for your cats to be properly cared for in your absence. So, you can rest assured that they will be just fine while you're gone. Though it may hurt to admit it, they probably won't even miss you.

As Spike puts it, "I'm staying here. And as long as I'm properly fed and admired, my servants [that's us mere humans] can go wherever they like!"

2: Puppy Pack Your Bags

It has been said that every successful vacation begins with careful packing. This is just as true for your dog as for yourself—you need to bring along the proper supplies. Use the handy checklist on p. 23 to be sure nothing important gets left behind.

Many of these supplies are as close as your local pet store. You can also check in dog magazines at your library or newsstand for the names of mail order pet supply houses and write or call for their catalogs. You'll be amazed at the variety of new gadgets available to make traveling with your pet easy and fun.

Collar and leash

Every dog should wear a sturdy leather or woven collar at all times, with the appropriate license, identification and rabies tags attached.

9

Don't use a choke collar as a permanent collar! Properly used, it can be helpful during training sessions, but if left on your dog all the time, the choke collar could snag on a low branch or other obstruction. Don't let your beloved pet become one of the many sad stories of dogs who choked to death when their owners were not there to rescue them.

If your dog is really hard to control, check with a reputable trainer about using a *prong collar* during your training sessions. This type of collar has blunt metal prongs that momentarily pinch the dog's neck, when he pulls against the leash or when you administer a *correction*. Again, this is for use during training sessions only; don't leave it on your dog all the time!

You'll need a 1-ft to 6-ft long leash for walking with your dog close to your side. Woven nylon or leather works better than metal chain, which is noisy and harder to hold onto. Also check out the new retractable leashes that extend to 16 feet or more so your pet can investigate his surroundings without dragging you every which way, and retract fully for close walking. Ginger does just fine with her bright red nylon collar and 6-ft leather leash.

🐕 Attending a basic obedience class with your dog is one of the very best ways to help him master the fine art of walking on leash.

All the proper ID tags

As important as your dog's license and ID tags are at home, they're even more vital when you travel. Should you and your pet lose track of each other, those ID tags will enable his finders to contact you. In addition to the permanent ID tag with your home address and phone number, I also recommend that you add a travel tag to your dog's collar showing where you can be reached *during* your trip if at all possible.

Dog license tag—Among the many other good reasons for licensing your dog, the license number and phone number of your county dog control department that appear on this tag represent another way to trace a lost dog's owner.

Permanent identification tag—This should list your name, home address and phone number, and perhaps your dog's name. (Ginger's tag even has her regular veterinarian's phone number.) Ideally, this information should be permanently engraved or stamped onto a metal tag. The rectangular style of tag that fastens flat to the collar stays cleaner and doesn't add to the jingling of the other tags.

Any number of companies can create permanent ID tags for you. Veterinary offices often have ordering information from several of them. Dog magazines are full of ads for this service—check your library or newsstand. Some mail order catalogs also offer them.

Rabies tag—Provided by your veterinarian. This tag bears a serial number that can be traced back to the veterinarian and then to the dog's owner. There could be dire consequences if your dog were to get picked up as a stray, or (heaven forbid) bite someone, and not have proof of current rabies vaccination.

Travel tag—Very important! This tag shows where you can be reached *during your vacation*. Check your pet store for a two-part tag consisting of a paper liner you can write on, that fits inside a clear plastic case. You can also get a barrel-type tag that unscrews to hold a rolled-up slip of paper—just be sure to tighten the two halves together *very securely* to keep them from separating accidentally.

Write or type the name, address, city and phone number where you're staying. If your trip includes several destinations, either list them all or prepare a separate slip for each destination—then be sure to update the tag at your next destination. As an alternative, list the name and phone number of someone who can receive messages for you.

Also write "Reward Offered" (no specific dollar amount) and "Call collect, or we will reimburse your phone expenses" on the tag.

Microchip ID system

Microchipping is one of the newest and most promising ways to identify a lost pet. While tags or collars can fall off or be removed, a microchip stays with your pet forever. Each chip is programmed with a unique code that can be detected by a hand-held scanner, similar to the ones used in retail stores.

Microchip scanners are now used at thousands of animal control agencies, shelters and veterinary clinics across the country. Once the chip's code has been retrieved, the staff simply calls it in to the national database agency, which is accessible 24 hours a day, 365 days a year through a toll-free number. The database agency immediately notifies you that your dog has been found.

Your veterinarian can implant the microchip, no bigger than a grain of rice, beneath your pet's skin in a safe, quick office procedure. Then all you have to do is register your pet's unique code and your contact information with the national database agency to receive coverage anywhere you travel in the U.S.

The cost of implanting the microchip and the one-time fee to register your pet in the database add up to about $50—pretty inexpensive insurance for your dog's safe return if he should ever get lost.

Health certificate

Get this certificate from your veterinarian not more than 10 days before beginning your trip. Effective for 30 days, it states that your pet is in good health and lists his current vaccinations. While not strictly required within Oregon when traveling by car, you'll *definitely* need this if you plan to travel by air (even just in-state) or to enter Canada. Before traveling to any other countries, check with their embassies for specific vaccinations and other requirements.

If your pet takes medication or has other problems, get a copy of his medical records along with the health certificate. Make sure the paperwork includes your veterinarian's name, address and phone number, in case follow-up information is needed.

The most well known canine vaccination is for rabies, which is required every three years in Oregon. In fact, you can't get a dog license without proof of a current rabies vaccination. And as a caring, responsible pet owner, *of course* you license your dog, right?

In addition, your pet should be immunized against distemper, hepatitis, parainfluenza, leptospirosis and possibly parvo. Depending on where you'll be traveling, your veterinarian may also recommend a preventive for heartworm or Lyme disease.

Also ask about annual booster shots for corona and bordetella. These safeguard your pet against catching something nasty from other dogs, such as kennel cough, and are often required before your dog can attend obedience classes. And you'll be prepared in case you ever have to temporarily place him in a boarding kennel, since many kennels won't accept dogs without proof of these vaccinations.

Bottom line on vaccinations: Your traveling dog is exposed to many new health hazards at rest stops, parks and other public areas. Along with the stress of drinking unfamiliar water and meeting new dogs, these factors add up to very real dangers for the non-vaccinated dog. So be safe—vaccinate!

🐕 Some vaccines can take up to 30 days to develop their full protective strength, so check with your veterinarian and *plan ahead*!

First aid kit

A basic first aid kit is easy to put together and enables you to deal with emergencies until you can get to a local veterinarian. You'll find a list of the items that belong in your first aid kit on pp. 51–52.

Of course you'll also bring along any special medication your veterinarian may have prescribed. If fleas are a problem in the area you're visiting, you may want to include flea-and-tick spray or powder—just be sure to apply it to your dog only when outdoors, never in your motel room.

Travel crate

Many trainers, breeders and veterinarians recommend using a dog carrier, or *crate*, when your dog travels in the car. Obviously, this is more practical with small dogs than with larger ones—it is much easier to fit a Beagle-sized crate into the back seat than one large enough for a Rottweiler.

Several types of crate are available, from collapsible wire mesh panels to heavy molded plastic. A wire crate works especially well in the flat back of a van or station wagon, while the plastic carriers fit better into the back seat of a sedan. Of course, when traveling by plane, your dog *must* be in an airline-approved travel crate.

The crate should be large enough for your dog to turn around, lie down, and stand or sit up without hitting his head. Even if yours is still a puppy, get a crate that will be large enough for his full adult size. However, this is your dog's den, so think *cozy* and *secure*—don't get anything larger than necessary.

To cushion and provide traction underfoot, place a folded blanket on the bottom of the crate. Better yet, cut a thick piece of carpet to fit snugly without slipping—ask your local carpet dealer for a remnant or sample square.

Restraints and safety barriers

If a travel crate isn't the answer for your situation, not to worry—there are a number of other safety options you can use instead for a car-traveling dog.

Seat belts—Available for dogs of all sizes, these consist of a chest harness and a strap that fastens to the car seat or to the regular seat belt. These allow your dog to either sit up or lie down in the passenger seat, yet prevent him from being thrown forward in the event of a sudden stop. Various size ranges and types are available.

Metal barriers—These allow you to close off the back seat, or the back of a station wagon. These may be either temporarily or permanently installed. Your dog can see and hear you through the barrier, but is securely restrained from jumping or being thrown into the front seat.

Elastic mesh nets—These nets create a barrier between front and back seats and can be ordered for specific makes of cars. They prevent your dog from jumping into the front seat. Stretch nets are also available in generic sizes and shapes to fit most car models. These have elastic bands that fasten to special hardware installed on the interior of the car.

Collapsible window screens—Made of strong plastic struts that expand like a child's safety gate, these fit securely into a partially opened car window. With screens in place on both sides of the car, there is plenty of air circulation but no danger of your dog jumping out—or of someone reaching into the parked car. When removed, the screens take up almost no space and fit easily under a car seat.

Food

First and foremost, you'll need to bring along dog food and a bowl to serve it in. Unless you are absolutely certain that your dog's preferred brand of food is available wherever you plan to travel, pack enough dog food for the entire trip.

If your dog typically nibbles at his food without finishing it all right away, bring a bowl with a snap-on lid that can go back into your dog's tote bag without spilling kibble all over. The shallow containers used for whipped toppings or margarine work very well.

You may also want to bring along a vinyl placemat for catching spills under the food and water bowls.

This is an item you can pick up for pennies at garage or rummage sales. Or you can get really fancy mats and bowls in pet stores or mail order catalogs.

Remember to pack a can opener for canned food, along with a serving spoon and a snap-on lid for covering any portion to be saved for the next meal. If your dog is accustomed to frequent dog treats or snacks, pack those too. And a small cooler may be helpful in hot weather for keeping drinking water or leftover canned food cool.

Water

Pack a plastic gallon jug of water and an unbreakable bowl where they'll be accessible during your travels, since your dog will need a drink of water every few hours. Don't let him drink from streams or puddles—drinking unfamiliar or polluted water can lead to stomach upsets and diarrhea. Also, *never* allow your dog to drink from the toilet in your motel room—some establishments put cleaning products into the toilet tank, which could make him very sick.

Many veterinarians recommend bringing enough water from home to last at least halfway through your trip. By gradually mixing your own water with the local tap water, you can prevent an unpleasant reaction. You can also buy distilled water for less than a dollar a gallon at most grocery stores.

Bedding & towels

You should always travel with your dog's own bed and cleanup towels. Your dog will thank you—and so will the hotel and motel managers, for sparing their furnishings. If your dog is accustomed to sleeping on the bed with you, or on other furniture, bring a sheet from home to protect the bedspread or upholstery. And do consider training your dog to stay off the furniture, at home *and* when traveling.

A travel crate, so useful in the car, also makes the perfect bed. It is reassuringly cozy and safe. If you're not using a crate, then bring along a *familiar* washable blanket or other bedding. Ginger travels with the same trusty sleeping bag that she sleeps on at home. Zipped up and folded in half, it makes a thick, soft bed. Opened out full length, it protects the back seat of the car from dirt, mud and beach sand.

An absolute must is a pair of towels especially for your dog. Use these to rub down a wet coat or wipe muddy or sandy paws. Spread one out under the water bowl if your dog is an enthusiastic drinker.

The sheet, dog towels, and bedding can all be found very inexpensively at garage sales, rummage sales, or second hand stores. Ginger's sleeping bag cost a dollar, and her towels were a quarter apiece. The tote bag which holds her travel supplies was another garage sale find—all for less than three dollars.

20

Grooming aids

Pack your dog's brush or comb, since you'll probably be going to places that are fun but will result in
a dirty or sandy dog. A quick brushing *before* going
back indoors will go a long way toward keeping your
motel room fresh and endearing you to the house-
keeping staff. Not to mention how much your pet
probably enjoys being groomed. Ginger jumps up
and down with delight at the mere sight of her brush.

Take care of major grooming chores *before* your
trip—trim those too-long toenails and brush the
loose hair out of his coat. And pack that bottle of pet
shampoo if he has a tendency to roll in smelly things.
I'll never forget the time one of my husband's dogs
found a dead seal on the beach—'nuff said!

Cleaning up

Many hotels and motels lay out free amenities such
as shampoo and hand lotion. Wouldn't it be great if
they offered guests with dogs the choice of a few
disposable pooper scoopers instead! In the mean-
time, however, it is up to us as dog owners to take
full responsibility for cleaning up after our dogs.

Please, please be considerate of others by cleaning up
after your dog's rest stops—whether in a park, on
the motel grounds, or at a highway rest stop.

You can use either disposable pooper scoopers, or a reusable scooper with disposable bags—plus another bag for storing the scooper between uses.

For a low cost, "low tech" method, use a plastic produce bag saved from a trip to the grocery store. Place your hand inside the bag and use this "glove" to pick up the doggy doo. With your other hand, turn the bag inside out, then twist the top shut and secure it with a knot. Properly dispose of the bag in a trash can.

Keep several clean, folded bags in your car, ready for the next rest stop. And *always* tuck one in your pocket when taking your dog out for a walk. Zip-top plastic bags also work well.

🐕 The true Cadillac of disposable pooper scoopers is called the Dispoz-A-Scoop, made by PetPro Products, Inc. 504 North Oak Street, Inglewood CA 90302 (1-800-873-5957). It consists of a small plastic bag with a wire rim and a cardboard handle that neatly slides down the wire to become a lid, for a completely hands-free pickup.

Even seasoned canine travelers occasionally have car sickness accidents, so it's a good idea to pack supplies in the car for quick cleanups. Paper towels, pre-moistened towelettes, or a wet washcloth in a plastic bag are all good. Stash them in an easy-to-reach spot in the car, such as under the front seat.

Last but not least—a flashlight

Keep one in the car and another in your dog's tote bag so it will be handy when you leave the motel room for those just-before-bedtime walks.

Tote bag checklist

- First aid kit, health certificate/medical records

- Dog bed (sleeping bag or blanket) and towels

- Dog food, bowl, serving spoon, can opener and snap-on lid, vinyl placemat

- Jug of water, drinking bowl

- Dog brush or comb, shampoo

- Pooper scoopers (reusable or disposable) or a supply of plastic bags

- Paper towels, pre-moistened towelettes, or wet washcloth in a plastic bag

- Flashlight

- One or two favorite chew toys!

3: Good Behavior is a TEAM Effort

Which sort of pet would you rather vacation with: a barky, uncontrollable bundle of energy, or a well-behaved traveler? The answer is obvious, and basic obedience training is the key.

"Obedience" simply means that your dog is reliably under your control, both on and off the leash. Mastering just a few useful commands—and reviewing them often with your pet— can make all the difference in his behavior.

What commands are necessary?

According to noted dog trainer Bruce Sessions, only two commands are truly required for the traveling dog: *come* and *no*. Check your local library for his excellent article "Training the RV Dog" in the September 1985 issue of *Trailer Life* magazine. He explains how to teach these vital commands in just 15 minutes a day for one week. The practice sessions can be fun for both you and your dog, and they help to strengthen the bond between the two of you.

Ginger and I have also learned a few more commands in obedience class that come in very handy: *sit, down, stay* and *heel.* Does your dog absolutely have to know all these commands before he can travel with you? No, but they will definitely make your trips less harried and more relaxed. Compare the following two scenarios...

Before obedience training

It was early morning at the motel, and I had just let Ginger off her leash (my first mistake) in a far corner of the motel grounds for a relief stop. Another guest and her dog suddenly appeared and Ginger ran to investigate the newcomer, ignoring my call to *"Come back here right now!"* I had to chase Ginger and grab her by the collar. The other guest glared indignantly as our two dogs bristled and snarled at each other in the traditional "I'm a tougher dog than you are" dance. On the leash again, Ginger lunged along the path at full speed, dragging me behind her.

In the motel room, Ginger ran back and forth between the window and the closed door, barking at the sounds of people and cars outside—in spite of my repeated scolding to *"Stop that barking and lie down."* Loaded down with luggage, I opened the door and she ran out ahead of me, nearly tripping another guest in her excitement.

And after

Let's try this again now that Ginger and I have completed our obedience classes: I take her outside *on the leash* for her morning rest stop. If she moves toward an approaching dog, I tell her *"Heel"* and we walk in the opposite direction. If she makes any aggressive move or sound, I say *"No!"* sharply and we keep walking—without her pulling on the leash.

Back in the motel room, if Ginger barks at a sound outside, I say *"No!"* followed by *"Down."* She lies down quietly on her own bed. When checking out of the room, I put her on the leash *before* opening the door, tell her *"Heel"* and she walks politely beside me to the car. Once she's safely inside, I retrieve the luggage and finish loading the car.

What a difference!

Feel the difference in stress levels between these two scenarios? And that's just the beginning of the day—imagine an entire weekend trip with an uncontrollable dog versus a well-behaved traveler.

Obedience 101

You *can* learn about obedience training from books, and there are some excellent ones available. See pp. 251–253 for a list of my favorites.

However, I definitely recommend that you and your dog attend at least a beginners' obedience class. A trained instructor can get you off to a great start and help to avoid behavior problems before they begin.

Professional dog trainers usually offer both group and one-on-one sessions—check the Yellow Pages under "Dog Training." Beginning, intermediate and advanced levels of obedience classes may also be available through your local school district or community college. Call the school office and ask about their Continuing Education or Community Education programs. Class schedules may also be available at the Post Office or your local bank.

🐾 Ginger's favorite class is conducted by trainer and pet innkeeper Susie Osborn at *Susie's Country Inn for Dogs & Cats* in Vancouver, WA. Located not far from the Portland International Airport, this is also where Ginger stays when we must travel without her. Call *Susie's* at 360/576-K9K9 for information about obedience classes or boarding your pet.

Train BEFORE you travel

The time to begin obedience training is *before* your trip—so that your dog can learn the basic commands in a controlled area without distractions. Once he understands the commands, start practicing with him in a public area like a park, surrounded by people and other dogs. He'll soon learn that you expect the same good behavior wherever he goes with you.

Relax and have fun with this training time. Your dog will love the extra attention you lavish on him, and he'll try to please you. Be patient and upbeat even if he gets confused at first. If you reach a stumbling block, go back to an earlier command that he knows well to get his confidence level back up. Then try the more difficult command again.

Keep your training sessions short so that they don't turn into torture for either one of you. And always end with a few minutes of plain old playing—toss a ball for your dog to fetch, or lead him on a run around the yard to release any leftover tension. After all, good behavior is supposed to make your time together more fun, right?

Basic commands

The following discussion is based on the collective expertise of a number of well-known trainers and authors. For more detailed information on training, check your local bookstore or library for their books (listed in the back of this guide).

Come—This is an easy command that most dogs pick up very quickly. You want to get your dog's attention in such an inviting way that there's nothing else he'd rather do than come running to you. While your dog is on a leash or long cord, call his name followed by the command *"Come."* As soon as he starts toward you, praise him lavishly. Giving a small food treat at first for every positive response helps to reinforce the idea that coming when called is a wonderful idea.

No—There is no specific routine for teaching this command. Just belt it out in a very firm tone of voice, whenever your dog is doing something you *really* don't want him to do. Don't overuse it though—save it for when he does something you absolutely will not tolerate; otherwise you risk losing its impact. The sudden loud command should startle him out of whatever he's doing. Then as soon as he begins to pay attention to you, praise him. You may even want to call him over to you for a pat on the head or a good ear-scratching.

Sit—With your dog on the leash, say his name and then *"Sit."* At the same time, pull up gently on the leash and push down on his hindquarters to guide him into the sit position. Praise him (*"Good sit"*) and then release him from this position with *"Okay"* or *"Release."* Only after you give the release command is he is allowed to stand up again. Then give lots of praise, both verbal and hands-on. Most dogs will be so delighted with themselves by now that they'll happily repeat this exercise over and over as long as you keep telling them how wonderful they are.

Down—With your dog on the leash, say his name and the command *"Down"* while you pull downward on his leash. At first, you may also need to push down on his hindquarters or shoulders until he is lying down. Again, give lots of praise to reassure him that he's doing well, even if he immediately wants to stand up again. Use patience and lots of repetition here.

Stay—With your dog in the Sit or Down position, hold your hand in front of his face, palm toward him, while saying *"Stay."* Praise lavishly for even the shortest compliance, then release. Gradually increase the time your dog is expected to hold this position, then practice staying while you step further and further away. Always remember to release him from this position before going on to another command or ending the practice session, so he doesn't get the idea that *he* can decide when this command is over!

Heel (walking on leash)—Start with your dog sitting at your left side, leash in your left hand. Say his name, then give the command *"Heel"* just before you step out with your left foot. Take just a few steps the first time, then say *"Sit"* as you stop walking. You want him to learn to stay right beside you, and to immediately sit down when you stop.

Say *"Heel"* and start walking again, and so on. He'll soon learn to follow your steps. In fact, he'll probably anticipate your takeoff and start too soon at first, so be patient. Once he catches on to the routine, stop giving the Sit command every time, so that he learns to do it automatically.

Try carrying a small food treat right in front of his nose to keep him at your side rather than rushing ahead. Give him the treat after you walk a few steps and then stop. And of course, give lots of praise. (If you think this is starting to sound like the secret to obedience training—you're absolutely right!)

Controlling aggression

If you intend to take your well-behaved traveler out in public, he must be reliably *not* aggressive toward people or dogs. Some dogs don't start out being comfortable with other dogs. Their reactions range from defensive postures like raised fur along the back of the neck and fierce stares to outright barking or growling.

The best way to overcome defensive or aggressive tendencies is to get your dog accustomed to the presence of other dogs at an early age. Simply attending obedience classes will go a long way toward helping him relax around dogs and people. Your instructor can also offer specialized help for problem dogs.

The most important step in preventing aggression is to *always* have your dog under your control—this means on the leash—whenever you venture outside your car or motel room. Dog behaviorists say that once you establish yourself as "pack leader,"your dog will follow your lead on whether to charge ahead or hold back.

Ginger has always been uncomfortable around other dogs. She was apparently kept indoors for the first year of her life and didn't develop the normal doggy socializing skills. When I adopted her as a stray at the local Humane Society shelter, she was very defensive toward the other dogs there. A few months later, she was viciously attacked by two neighbor dogs, one of whom she had previously played with most amiably—which made her even more suspicious of other dogs.

Several obedience classes later, Ginger is still standoffish when meeting new dogs, but she has become pals with a few familiar dogs belonging to friends and neighbors. On the other hand, she is a total people-lover, going happily from person to person to be petted. It doesn't matter to her whether they

are longtime friends or first-time acquaintances—
she adores all kinds of people.

If your dog is a barker

Simply put, barking is *not* to be tolerated. A barking
dog makes everyone around you miserable. If you
are in your motel room and someone knocks on the
door, a single "alarm bark" is acceptable, but no more
than that. You should train your dog to stop barking
as soon as you give the all-purpose command *"No!"*

A really insistent barker may need more than a spo-
ken command to break through his mental barriers. I've had good luck with plain water in a plastic
squirt bottle. One good squirt in the face doesn't hurt
your dog, but it certainly interrupts his train of
thought, especially when accompanied by a loud
"No!" and followed with praise as soon as he stops
barking.

Of course, a dog left behind in a motel room, barking incessantly, is absolutely out. Barking like that
is a sign of stress, as in "They left me here all alone
and I'm scared/bored/frustrated." It isn't fair to your
dog any more than it is to the unfortunate neighbors who have to endure the noise.

Never leave your dog alone in the motel room. He
should be going with you—isn't that why you

brought him on the trip in the first place? If you must leave him for a short time, while you're in a restaurant for example, let him wait in your car, not in the room.

If you already use a travel crate, your dog should be accustomed to sitting or lying down quietly when he's inside it. Put him in the crate for a few minutes to calm down when he becomes upset and barky. Be sure to practice this "time-out in the crate" exercise at home before you travel, so that your dog knows exactly what is expected of him when he is put into his little den.

Learning to love car rides

Many dogs just naturally love going anywhere in the car with you, but others have difficulty getting used to the sound and motion. A few advance preparations will help to ensure a comfortable trip for all concerned.

Getting used to the car—Jumping around in the car, drooling, panting excessively or throwing up are all signs that your dog is nervous about being in the car. A few practice rides can help to reassure him that riding in the car can be fun rather than intimidating. In extreme cases, you may need to start by sitting quietly with him in the car, not even starting the engine. Ignore him for a few minutes—read a

35

magazine article or two—then let him out of the car with a simple word of praise and a pat on the head.

Repeat this exercise until he can enter the car, sit quietly, and exit without any upset. Then try starting the car but not going anywhere. Next, try driving around the block and back home again, and so on. By the time you've progressed to taking him with you on short errands, such as to the grocery store and back, he'll probably just fall asleep.

Arrange some of your practice trips to include a fun destination or activity, like a brisk walk in the park. Ginger loves going to the drive-up bank window with me, because, believe it or not, the teller always has a bowl of doggy treats handy!

Avoiding a "nervous stomach"—Stress can trigger car sickness, so don't give food or water for at least an hour before a practice ride. Allow time for a few minutes of exercise and a chance to relieve himself just before you leave. If he still gets carsick, see pp. 71–72 for some simple remedies.

Riding politely—Train your dog to sit or lie down quietly—no jumping around, and no barking in your ear or out the window. You may want to use one of the safety restraints described on pp. 17–18.

Loading and unloading—For his own safety, your dog *must* learn to wait for your command before getting into or out of the car. Never open the door without checking that the leash is attached to his collar, and that you have a firm grasp on the other end of the leash. Losing control of an excited dog in unfamiliar territory can be disastrous—so use the Stay command to keep him safely in the car until you are ready for him to get out.

Reviewing what your dog already knows

A brief practice session makes a great exercise break during your trip. It also helps to reinforce the idea that obedience is expected even with lots of unfamiliar distractions.

When you stop at a rest area, a park or other open area, start by walking your dog on the leash. Pause a few times to have him sit or lie down, then release him and continue your walk. Or tell him to sit and stay while you walk ahead a few steps—still holding the leash, of course. Then call him to you once more, and so on.

A few minutes of this activity at each rest stop will leave you with a happy dog who settles down politely—and will probably even fall asleep—as soon as you start driving again.

4: The Well-Behaved Traveler Hits the Road

Okay, you've faithfully completed your dog's obedience training, assembled his first aid kit and packed his food, water, and other traveling supplies. You've made your advance room reservations, you're ready to go, and your ecstatic pet is running in circles around the car. This is the payoff for all your preparations—it's time to hit the road!

Tips for traveling in the car

The safest way for a smaller dog to ride in the car is in a travel crate. This protects him in case of a sudden stop and keeps him from jumping around in the car or getting underfoot while you're trying to drive. If your pet is too large for a travel crate, consider using a doggy seat belt that offers similar protection but still allows him to sit or stand up. Whatever form of restraint you decide on, make sure your pet knows that he must stay in his assigned location in the car until you release him. Ginger's travel spot is on her sleeping bag, which has been spread out across the back seat to protect the upholstery.

If your pet is a nervous traveler, reassure him by remaining calm yourself. Praise him for sitting politely in his assigned spot, then ignore him as long as he behaves himself. Don't keep asking anxiously if he's all right, or giving constant reassurance—that will just make him more nervous.

Don't leave your dog's leash attached to his collar while the car is in motion. If you should make a sudden stop, the leash could snag on a door handle or seat back and strangle him. So take the leash off once he's safely inside the car. Just be sure to put it on again *before* opening the car door to let him out.

Open the car window just wide enough for your dog to put his nose into the fresh air, not his whole face. Never let him hang his head out the window of a moving car—not only could he squeeze his whole body out if he decided to chase something, but airborne objects such as insects or flying gravel could injure his ears and eyes. Or the force of the wind could actually give him an earache.

40

It goes without saying that your pet belongs *inside* the vehicle. A dog riding in the back of an open pickup truck is an accident just waiting to happen. He is exposed to wind-borne hazards and harsh weather, and could be thrown out of the vehicle if you swerve or brake suddenly.

If you need to leave your dog in the parked car—while you stop for lunch, for example—be sure that he won't suffer from heat buildup on a warm day, which can lead to heatstroke or even death. Park under cover if you can, or at least in the shade. For cross ventilation, open one or more windows on each side of the car and insert the collapsible screens described on p. 18. Check frequently to be sure the temperature in the car is still comfortable.

Rest stop pointers

When traveling a long distance, stop every few hours to give both you and your pet a chance to stretch and relax. Keep him on the leash the whole time you're at the rest stop, and stay in the designated pet areas.

If you've been traveling for quite awhile or the weather is warm, he'll appreciate a drink of water. Then give him a few minutes to relieve himself and walk around a bit. Be considerate of others by *always* cleaning up after your dog—use plastic bags or pooper scoopers, and properly dispose of the waste in a garbage can.

This is a great time for a short exercise break, especially if you combine it with a review of obedience commands. Try walking a short distance and have him sit or lie down, then walk for another minute and practice a different command, and so on. A few minutes of activity will have you both feeling refreshed and ready to continue your trip.

Room etiquette

When you arrive at your overnight destination, be sure to remind the staff that your dog is traveling with you. Of course, you should already have stated this when making your advance reservation, but tell them again now that you have arrived. That way, they can be sure not to put you in a "no-pets" room by mistake—many establishments reserve certain rooms for guests who suffer from allergies. Sneaking a dog into a no-pets room hurts all dog owners by jeopardizing the management's willingness to accept dogs in the future.

Ask where on the grounds you can exercise your dog, whether or not they have disposable pooper scoopers available, and if there are designated trash cans you should use for disposal.

Place your pet's bed in an out-of-the-way spot in the room and show him where it is, then make sure that he uses his own bed and not the furniture.

If you allow your pet to sleep on your bed or other furniture at home, bring along one of your own sheets or blankets to cover the motel furnishings—and resolve to begin breaking that habit as soon as your trip is over. Every dog should have his own (washable) bed. Place it on the floor beside you so he's still close, but don't let him sleep on your bed.

If your dog gets bored or rambunctious in the room, offer him a favorite chew toy to play with. Watch that he doesn't damage the furnishings—remember, you are legally and financially responsible for any damage your dog does, both indoors and out.

While it's natural for dogs to bark at unfamiliar sounds, don't tolerate *any* barking in the room, no matter what's going on outside. Incessant barking is the single most common reason given by managers for not allowing dogs to stay.

N*ever* leave your pet alone in the room when you go out, for example, to dinner. Take him along and let him wait for you in the car rather than in the room. He'll feel safer in that familiar place and should settle right down for a nap while you're gone.

Mealtime arrangements

Put your dog's food and water bowls on a dog towel or vinyl placemat in the bathroom—its smooth floor is much easier to clean than the carpet in the main room. If your pet is an especially enthusiastic eater or slobbery drinker, it's easy to rinse the mat off and let it drip-dry in the bathtub. And don't let him drink out of the toilet—cleaning chemicals that may have been added to the water could make him sick.

On checkout day, it's a good idea to withhold food and water at least an hour before starting a long drive. If your pet tends to suffer from car sickness, you may need to do this as much as six hours before departure, meaning the night before if you plan to leave early in the morning.

Walking on the grounds

Shortly after eating or drinking, your dog will need a walk outside, in the designated pet relief area. This is also true after he has been waiting in the car while you were out having your own dinner. And of course, just before bedtime is another important walking time. Be sure to always take along the pooper scooper or plastic bag for cleaning up after him.

Before you and your dog leave the room, make him sit down by the door while you put his leash on. He

44

should remain sitting while you open the door and step outside, then he can follow you out. Don't let him charge through the door ahead of you.

You should always keep your dog leashed while on the premises, of course. And be courteous when taking him for a "relief walk"— use the designated pet area or at least go to the far end of the grounds, away from buildings, major footpaths and children's play areas. Don't let him romp in landscaped areas like flower beds, decorative ponds or streams. Basically, just be aware of your pet's energy level and potential for destruction, and seek out areas where he can play harmlessly.

When you and your pet return to the room, check him over before stepping inside. Use the dog towel you brought from home to wipe off any mud or sand on his feet. This small courtesy only takes a second, helps to keep the carpet clean, and has a definite effect on the manager's willingness to continue accepting pets as guests.

On the trail

When you go out for the day's activities, remember to bring along the doggy water jug and drinking bowl, just as you would pack your own water bottle for a hike. And of course, the first aid kit should be in your car, not left behind in the room.

Be aware of your pet's effect on other people and animals when you're out in public. You are responsible for making sure that he doesn't cause anyone else discomfort. If you're walking along a trail, for example, rein him in to walk closely beside you when you encounter other hikers. Don't let him monopolize the whole walkway or run up to greet them—or worse yet, to challenge their own pet.

Remember that although your dog is the apple of your eye, not everyone shares your enchantment. In fact, some people are very fearful of even the smallest, meekest dog. So keep your pet on the leash unless you're absolutely sure that no one else is around and that there is no local leash law prohibiting dogs running free. Even then, put the leash back on as soon as you encounter another person or animal. Many towns have enacted ordinances that require dogs to be on leash *at all times*, as do most city, state and national parks.

Watch out for potential hazards underfoot: broken glass, nails or other sharp objects, burning hot pavement, melted road tar, chemical sprays or wet paint could all injure his feet or poison him when he tries to lick them off his fur.

Also remember to clean his feet after walking on snow or ice that may have been treated with salt or other de-icing chemicals.

At the beach

Many dogs love playing in the ocean, and few scenes are more enjoyable to watch than a happy dog chasing waves up and down the beach. However, a naturalist friend has asked me to remind dog owners not to let their pets chase the shore birds, which can cause them to suffer severe or even fatal stress.

Keep a close eye on your pet while he's in the water—don't let him go out too far, as dangerous currents can arise suddenly and carry him away from shore.

Also watch that he doesn't drink too much salt water or he'll be throwing up in the car later. A little bit won't hurt him, and he'll soon learn that he doesn't like the taste after all. Just be sure to offer him a drink of fresh water when he gets back to the car. He may still need to throw up the salt water already in his stomach, so wait a few minutes before bundling him into the car.

After walking your dog on the beach, brush off any sand clinging to his feet or coat. Salt water that dries on his skin can cause lasting irritation, so rinse the salt away as soon as possible—definitely *before* returning to your room. This is where those dog towels you packed in his tote bag come in handy. And of course, the towels provided in your motel room should *never* be used for dogs!

47

5: When Your Dog Needs First Aid

Whether your pet sustains a minor scratch or a life-threatening injury, you need to know what first aid measures to take. Then, for all but the most minor problems, your immediate next step is to get him to the nearest veterinary clinic.

If you're not sure just how serious the problem is, call them—most clinics are happy to answer questions over the phone, and can give you exact directions for getting there if it becomes necessary.

Put together your dog's own first aid kit in advance and *always* bring it (and this book) along when he travels with you. Carry it in your car when you're out and about, not back in the motel room with the luggage.

Before first aid is needed

Read through this chapter *now* to get a basic idea of what you would need to do in an emergency, and how to use the supplies in the first aid kit.

Knowing your dog's healthy state will help you to recognize when something is wrong. Sit down on the floor with your dog—he'll love the attention!—and listen to his breathing. Place your palm on his chest just behind the elbow and feel his heartbeat. Check the size and color of his pupils, the color of his gums and tongue, and how warm his body feels normally.

In an emergency, refer to specific sections in this chapter for the proper first aid steps to take. Or better yet, have another person read the steps aloud to you while you perform them on your pet. As soon as you complete the emergency procedures, take him to a veterinary clinic, or at least give call them for further instructions.

🐕 It's a good idea to identify nearby veterinary clinics at your vacation destination *before* the need arises. See the list of 24 hour emergency clinics on pp. 248–249, or check your local Yellow Pages.

Your dog's first aid kit

This list includes the emergency supplies you'll need until you can get to the clinic. All items are available from your veterinarian or local pharmacy. The dosage of some medicines varies according to body weight, so write your pet's exact dose on a piece of masking tape attached to each medicine container.

Pack everything into a sturdy container, such as a fishing tackle box or one of the colorful new cosmetics travel cases.

Travel papers—copies of your dog's license, health certificate, veterinary records if he has special medical problems, and a master lost-and-found poster with extra photos of your dog as described on p. 78. Store all this paperwork in a zip-top plastic bag

Any medication your dog is currently taking— and a copy of the written prescription

Small packets of **honey**—available in restaurants, or **hard candies** (*but no chocolate*)

Antibacterial ointment—such as *Panalog* from your veterinarian, or *Neosporin* from any pharmacy

Tranquilizers—but *only* if prescribed by your veterinarian *and* you try out the recommended dose on your pet before the trip. The ASPCA recommends

51

against using tranquilizers because their effects can be unpredictable.

Plastic dosage spoon—to measure liquid medicines (available at any pharmacy, often for free).

Paper or **flexible plastic cup**—that you can squeeze into the shape of a pouring spout to administer liquid medicines.

Slip-on muzzle—the quick-release kind that fastens with hook-and-loop tape is especially easy to use.

Kaopectate
Hydrogen peroxide, 3% solution
Activated charcoal
Olive oil
Petroleum jelly
Sterile eye drops
Zip-top plastic bags
Sterile gauze pads
Adhesive tape and **elastic bandages**
Cotton-tipped swabs
Rectal thermometer
Ice pack
Tweezers
Pliers
Blunt-tipped scissors

Emergency stretcher—flat piece of wood or cardboard stored in your car's trunk (see p. 65).

Taking your dog's temperature

Have another person restrain your dog while you take his temperature, unless he's too weak to put up a fuss. Coat the rectal thermometer with a bit of petroleum jelly or hand lotion to make insertion easier.

Firmly grasp your dog's tail and very gently insert the thermometer about one inch while rotating it back and forth slightly. After one minute, remove it and read the temperature. Wash the thermometer with soap and *cool* water before returning it to its protective case. Normal body temperature is 100° to 101°—anything over 102.5° deserves a phone call to the veterinary clinic.

What to do in a life-threatening emergency

You have to give your pet the first aid he needs to survive until you reach a veterinarian. Remain calm and focused on what you need to do. Speak to him reassuringly while you work.

Each step listed here is described in greater detail in the sections that follow—exact page numbers are indicated for each step.

1. *Do not move him* until you have checked his injuries. The only exception is when it's unsafe to leave him where he is, such as in the middle of a busy street.

2. Check for a heartbeat—if there is none, start cardiac massage *immediately* (p. 57).

3. Check for breathing—if there is none, give him artificial respiration *immediately* (p. 57).

4. Muzzle and restrain him if he's in obvious pain, seems dazed or starts to struggle (p. 59).

5. Check for obvious injuries and take steps to control severe bleeding (p. 60).

6. Check for symptoms of internal bleeding (p. 61).

7. Check for signs of poisoning—depending on the type of poison, induce vomiting or make him swallow an antidote (p. 62).

8. Move him to your vehicle using a board, stiff cardboard or a blanket as a stretcher (p. 65).

9. Treat for shock by keeping him warm (p. 66).

10. Rush him to the nearest veterinary clinic. If possible, have another person call ahead so they can prepare for your pet's arrival.

If your dog is choking

The traveling dog may encounter chicken bones at picnic areas, fishing line at the river's edge—even more dangerous if a fishhook is still attached—or any number of other choking hazards that can be potentially fatal unless you act quickly.

Signs of choking include violent pawing at his mouth or throat and loud gasping or gagging sounds. In his panic, he may even bite your hand when you try to help.

If possible, have another person hold your pet while you open his mouth wide and pull his tongue out straight with your fingers or a cloth.

If you can see the entire object, pull it out. But *never* pull on a fishline that extends out of sight down his throat—there could be a hook at the other end. Instead, take him to a veterinary clinic for an x-ray.

If you can't see what he's choking on, place your hands on each side of his chest and squeeze in a sudden, forceful movement. The air expelled from his lungs may dislodge the object in his throat.

If he is still choking, head straight for the emergency clinic. Keep him as immobile as possible during the trip, and speak reassuringly to calm him.

If your dog is drowning

If your pet is in the water and can't make it back to shore, *do not* swim out to him. First, try to help him from shore by extending out a board, rope or any floating thing that he can hold or climb onto. If you still can't reach him, wade part of the way out and try again. If you absolutely must swim out to him, bring something he can cling to—otherwise you could be seriously clawed or even pulled under in his panic to get out of the water.

Once you get him onto the shore, clear any debris out of his mouth and lift his hind legs as high as possible to help drain his airway.

If his heart has stopped, start cardiac massage *immediately* (p. 57).

If he has a heartbeat but is not breathing, give artificial respiration *immediately* (p. 57).

Once he begins breathing on his own, dry him off and keep him warm. If he's willing to drink, give him warm liquids. If his body temperature doesn't quickly return to normal, check with a veterinarian for follow-up treatment.

Cardiac massage

Place your palm on your dog's chest just behind the elbow. (Practice this at home until you can easily detect his normal heartbeat.) If his heart has stopped beating, you have to restart it *right now*!

Gently lay your dog on his side with head extended—don't move him suddenly, as that can further deepen his shock. Pull his tongue out of his mouth to clear the airway.

Place your hands on each side of his chest just behind the elbow. Squeeze firmly and quickly to compress the chest and then release. Repeat once every second for 1 minute, then check for heartbeat again. If there still is none, repeat the steps above. As soon as his heart starts beating, give artificial respiration to restore his breathing.

Artificial respiration

Check your pet's heartbeat before beginning this procedure. If his heart has stopped, you must perform cardiac massage (see above) before giving artificial respiration.

If your dog has swallowed water while drowning or inhaled vomit or other liquids, lift his back legs as high above his head as possible for 15 seconds and give 3 or 4 downward shakes to drain his airway. Gently pull his tongue out and clear any debris out of his mouth with your hand or a cloth.

Place your hands on both sides of his chest just behind the elbow. Squeeze hard and then immediately release. Repeat once every 5 seconds for 1 minute.

If the movement of air into and out of the lungs seems blocked, open his mouth wide to see if an object is lodged in his throat, and remove it.

If he doesn't start breathing within 1 minute, grasp his muzzle firmly to hold his mouth shut. Take a deep breath, place your mouth over his nose forming an airtight seal, and blow gently. His chest should rise as the lungs expand.

Remove your mouth and listen for air leaving the lungs. Repeat every 5 seconds for 1 minute (10 to 15 breaths). Check to see if he's breathing on his own, then repeat for another 10 to 15 breaths and so on.

Have someone drive you and your dog to the veterinary clinic while you continue helping him to breathe. Don't give up even if there is no immediate response—dogs have been successfully revived after extended periods of artificial resuscitation, as long as the heart keeps beating.

Restraining an injured dog

An injured dog is also frightened, dazed, and in pain. He may not even recognize you, and may bite when you try to help him. Unless he's unconscious, you'll need to muzzle him before you can check his injuries.

Use the slip-on muzzle in your first aid kit or improvise one from a handkerchief, scarf, or his own leash—whatever is handy. Since a muzzle doesn't work well on a short-nosed dog, loosely place a coat or blanket over his head instead. Whatever you use, be sure not to restrict your dog's breathing. And be ready to remove the muzzle *immediately* if your dog starts to vomit or has trouble breathing.

Broken bones

If your dog is unable to move his leg or holds it at an odd angle, the bone may be fractured. Muzzle and restrain him before checking for broken bones, and handle the injured leg as little as possible. If the bone is protruding from the wound, cover with a clean cloth and control the bleeding with direct pressure.

If you can find a rigid stretcher (see p. 65) for moving your dog, don't waste time applying a splint. But if you have to jostle him in a blanket stretcher or carry him in your arms, you've got to immobilize the broken ends of the bone before moving him.

59

To apply a temporary splint, wrap a clean cloth around the leg for padding. Fold a newspaper, magazine or piece of cardboard in a U-shape around the leg or lay a strip of wood alongside it. Hold it all in place with adhesive tape or strips of cloth. The splint should extend beyond the joints above and below the fracture in order to hold the broken bones still.

External bleeding

Your first concern is to stop any major bleeding. Minor wounds that are losing only a small amount of blood can wait for the veterinarian. But if blood is spurting out or flowing steadily, you must act *now*.

Cover the wound with a sterile gauze pad or clean cloth if possible, or just place your hand directly over the source of the blood flow. Apply firm, steady pressure until the bleeding stops.

If the wound is on the leg or tail and you cannot slow down the blood loss after a few minutes of direct pressure, you must apply a tourniquet. This may result in having to amputate the appendage, so use this method only as a last resort—*always* try direct pressure first. And *never* place the tourniquet over a joint or a fractured bone.

Wrap a handkerchief or other strip of cloth in a loose loop around the leg about one inch above the wound.

Tie it with a double knot, then place a strong, short stick in the loop. Twist the stick to tighten the loop until the blood flow stops.

Now take him to the emergency clinic, *fast*. On the way to the clinic, you *must* loosen the tourniquet every 10 minutes to allow some blood to flow through the appendage. Apply direct pressure to the wound to prevent further bleeding, and tighten the tourniquet again only if absolutely necessary.

If you suspect internal bleeding

Hidden bleeding inside your dog's body can result from a traumatic blow, or from certain kinds of poison. Even if he has no visible wounds, his internal organs may be seriously damaged. He may go into fatal shock without immediate veterinary care.

Signs of internal bleeding include: pale skin, gums and tongue; bleeding from ears, mouth or anus; bloody vomit or stool; difficulty breathing; extreme sleepiness. Symptoms may appear right after the accident or hours later, even if he seemed fine initially.

Use a rigid stretcher (see p. 65) if at all possible to move your dog to and from your car on the way to the emergency clinic. Keep him warm and don't jostle him any more than you absolutely have to.

Poisoning

Your dog can be poisoned by eating or drinking a toxic substance, by inhaling it, by licking it off his coat or paws or by absorbing it through his skin.

Poisons your pet might encounter when traveling include spilled antifreeze, toxic bait put out for insects or rodents (or their dead bodies), garbage that contains poisonous substances or chemical sprays on plants that your dog chews or rolls in. Even your own prescription medicine can poison your pet if he discovers it in the motel room and accidentally swallows some while playing with this new "toy."

Symptoms of poisoning include: drooling or difficulty swallowing; trembling; cringing; abdominal pain or vomiting; rapid, shallow breathing; twitching; coma.

Contact poisoning

Rinse his coat *immediately* with lots of water—fresh water, sea water, mud puddle by the side of the road—whatever it takes to dilute the chemical and wash it away. Wear rubber gloves if you can, to avoid getting the toxic chemicals on your hands. Then wash him with mild hand soap or dog shampoo and rinse thoroughly again with clean water. Repeat until all traces of the chemicals are removed.

Watch your pet closely over the next few hours. If his skin appears irritated or he shows any symptoms of internal poisoning, see or call a veterinarian.

Swallowed poisons

Your first step is to determine what kind of poison your pet has swallowed. If the product container is available, it may identify the ingredients, the antidote and whether or not to induce vomiting.

Depending on the type of poison, you must choose between two very different first aid treatments— see **Method A** and **Method B** on the following page.

If you can't identify the type of poison, examine your dog's mouth and throat. If the tissues look burned or raw, treat for acid/alkali poisoning—Method A.

Try to collect a sample of the poison in one of the zip-top plastic bags from your first aid kit, or bring the poison container itself if at all possible. Also collect some of the material your dog vomits up. These samples will help the veterinarian identify the exact antidote your dog needs.

Then take him to the nearest veterinary clinic immediately!

Method A. When the poison IS an acid, alkali, or petroleum product:
DO NOT INDUCE VOMITING!
These extremely corrosive poisons will injure your dog's throat and mouth even more if he throws up.

Rinse his mouth with water to wash away any remaining chemicals. Make him swallow 2 to 3 tablespoons of olive oil or up to a cup of milk.

Keep him warm with a blanket or coat while you rush him to the nearest veterinary clinic.

Method B. When the poison is NOT an acid, alkali, or petroleum product:
INDUCE VOMITING IMMEDIATELY!
Mix equal parts of hydrogen peroxide and water. Make him swallow $1\frac{1}{2}$ tablespoonfuls of this mixture for every 10 pounds of body weight.

> Example: the dose for a 60-lb dog would be 6 x $1\frac{1}{2}$ = 9 tablespoons.

If he doesn't vomit within 10 minutes, repeat this dosage, but not more than three doses altogether.

After he vomits, make him swallow a mixture of 3 to 4 tablespoonfuls of activated charcoal in a cup of warm water.

Keep him warm with a blanket or coat while you rush him to the nearest veterinary clinic.

A special warning about antifreeze— sweet but deadly

Every year, dogs die from drinking antifreeze that dripped onto the ground from leaking car radiators, or was spilled by careless humans. This coolant has a sweet smell and taste that attracts many pets to try it—but even a tiny spoonful can be deadly.

If your dog has swallowed even the tiniest amount of antifreeze, induce vomiting *immediately* and rush him to a veterinarian for an antidote injection—but you must work *fast*. Minutes can make the difference between losing him or saving his life.

🐕 Pet-safe antifreeze is now available at auto supply stores and some service centers; ask for it the next time you have the radiator fluid in your car changed!

Moving an injured dog

The safest way to move your pet is on a *stretcher*, a flat rigid surface that won't flex under his weight. A piece of wood, heavy cardboard will do, or even an air mattress blown up as firm as you can make it. If that's unavailable, use a blanket, tarp or piece of clothing that you can carry by its corners to make as flat a surface as possible.

Slide your dog onto the stretcher without twisting or shaking him. If possible, have a helper lift his hindquarters and abdomen at exactly the same moment that you lift his head and shoulders.

If you are alone and can't find a rigid stretcher, you'll have to carry him in your arms. Place one arm around his hindquarters and the other around his front legs at the shoulder, supporting his head on your arm. Keep his spine as straight as possible.

Treating for shock

Shock is a sudden collapse of your dog's circulatory system brought on by sudden injury or other trauma. Be very careful not to jostle or quickly move him— any rapid movement can bring on the *fatal* stages of shock.

Symptoms of shock include: extreme muscle weakness; loss of bladder and bowel control; shallow, rapid breathing and pulse; pale or whitish gums and mouth; body feels cold; appears asleep or semiconscious.

Pull his tongue straight forward to clear the airway— be very cautious, as even the most gentle dog may bite when dazed from great pain or fear. Try to get his head lower than his body to encourage circulation. However, if he has a head injury, keep his head level with his body.

Cover him with a warm blanket or coat—unless the shock is caused by heatstroke and his temperature is already too high. Now take him to a veterinarian for follow-up care, and have someone call ahead so they can prepare for the emergency procedures he will need as soon as he gets there.

Treating burns

Watch for hazards that can lead to your dog being accidentally burned: sparks from a beach bonfire, boiling hot liquids spilled from a tiny kitchen unit, licking meat juices from a hot barbecue grill or brushing against a space heater. Chewing on an electrical cord can lead to burns in the mouth as well as unconsciousness, shock, and even death—be sure to *unplug the cord* before touching your dog.

If the burned skin is red but not broken, run cold water over it, or cover with an ice pack or a cold wet towel. If the burned area is heavily blistered, raw, weeping or bleeding, blackened or whitish, *do not apply ice or water*—just cover with a sterile gauze pad or clean cloth. Treat for shock (see p. 66) and get your dog to the nearest veterinarian *immediately*.

67

Minor cuts and scrapes

When Ginger is on the trail of a squirrel (though she never catches them) she'll gleefully charge into the thickest blackberry patch. She returns covered with thorns and scratches—grinning like a fool and enormously pleased with herself. So I've gotten plenty of practice at removing stickers and cleaning up her scrapes and scratches.

I have a running joke with Ginger's regular veterinarian that the next time she needs stitches for a torn-up ear—which means shaving a bald strip around the ear to keep fur out of the wound as it heals—we're going to give her a gold earring to go with her Mohawk haircut.

Rinse away any dirt in your pet's wound with clean water, then swab with hydrogen peroxide. If it's still bleeding, cover with a gauze pad and apply pressure until the bleeding stops. Then lightly apply an antibiotic ointment such as *Panalog* or *Neosporin.*

If the wound is large or your dog just won't leave it alone, cover with a gauze pad held in place with adhesive tape or an elastic bandage. And of course, for anything more than a minor scratch or scrape, you should have a veterinarian take a look at it.

Removing foreign objects

Use common sense in deciding whether or not to try removing an embedded object such as a burr or porcupine quill. In some cases, incorrect removal can do more harm than if you just keep your dog as motionless as possible while taking him straight to the nearest clinic to let the veterinarian do the job.

From the ears—Use tweezers to gently remove seeds or burrs from the *outer* ear canal. If your dog still shakes his head or scratches repeatedly at his ear, seeds may also be deeper inside the ear canal and must be removed by a veterinarian.

From the eyes—If your pet paws at his eye or rubs his face along the ground, gently hold the eyelid open and check for seeds or debris. To wash away a loose object, apply sterile eye drops. Don't try to remove an object that is embedded into the eye's surface. Instead, take him to the nearest veterinary clinic *right away.*

From everywhere else—You're already familiar with this routine if your dog loves to crash through the underbrush like Ginger does. Run your hands gently over his face, body and feet to check for thorns. If he's limping or holding up his paw, he's already zeroed in on the problem for you.

Use tweezers to pull out embedded stickers. If there's any bleeding or tearing of the skin, swab with hydrogen peroxide. When a foreign object is buried too deeply to find, either soak the affected body part in salt water (1 teaspoon salt per cup of lukewarm water) several times a day until the object works its way up to the surface where you can remove it, or else have a veterinarian remove it to begin with.

Remove sharp objects—such as porcupine quills or a fishhook—with pliers. Begin by using the wire cutter notches at the center of the pliers to clip off each porcupine quill tip, or the barbed point of the fishhook *if it is exposed.* When finished, rinse all the wounds with hydrogen peroxide. But if the fishhook point is hidden below the skin surface, or your dog won't submit to having the quills pulled out, take him straight to a veterinarian.

And watch out for ticks—Examine your dog closely after outdoor activities, especially his head, shoulders and feet. Forget the old wives' tales about using a match to burn the tick off, applying gasoline or petroleum jelly to make it let go, and so on. However, dousing the tick with alcohol or nail polish remover *may* make it easier to remove.

Use tweezers to grab the tick by its head, very close to the dog's skin, and firmly pull it out. Don't squeeze its fat abdomen—doing so might force disease-carrying blood back into the bite wound.

70

Above all, *don't use your fingers.* Ticks can carry Lyme disease and Rocky Mountain spotted fever, both of which are dangerous to humans. Swab the bite area with hydrogen peroxide. If the skin becomes red or irritated, see a veterinarian for follow-up treatment.

Treating an upset stomach

Car sickness is one of the most common complaints for the traveling dog—whether it's because he's fearful of the car, or just overly excited about coming along. Try reducing his stress level with practice rides as described on p. 35. Don't give food or water for at least an hour before traveling. And always allow him a few minutes of exercise and a last-minute chance to relieve himself.

If your dog still gets carsick, give him a small spoonful of honey, a piece of hard candy or a spoonful of plain vanilla ice cream to calm his stomach. *However, you should never give your dog any food containing chocolate, as it can be toxic!*

If these simple remedies don't help, ask your regular veterinarian about stronger medicines for motion sickness.

An upset stomach can also be caused by eating unfamiliar or spoiled food, or drinking unfamiliar water—contaminants in the water or a different mineral content can throw your pet's system for a loop. Give him 2 teaspoons of Kaopectate for each ten pounds of body weight, once every four hours. If the problem doesn't clear up within a day, this may be a symptom of a more serious illness, so take him to a veterinarian.

Treating diarrhea

This may be a temporary upset caused by the stress of unfamiliar surroundings, food or water, or a symptom of a more serious illness. Give 2 teaspoons of Kaopectate per ten pounds of body weight, once every four hours.

See a veterinarian if the diarrhea doesn't clear up within a day or if other symptoms appear, such as labored breathing, bloody stool, either a rise or drop in body temperature, listlessness or loss of appetite.

Dealing with heat problems

Summer can mean added hazards for your pet. Short haired dogs can be sunburned just as easily as people can. Older or overweight pets are more prone to heat problems, as are short-nosed breeds and dogs who are taking certain medications. Heat problems are even more likely if the humidity is also high.

When walking your dog, pay special attention to the surface underfoot—if it's too hot for your bare feet, then it's too hot for your dog's paws as well.

Heatstroke can be caused by too much exercise in the hot sun, not drinking enough water, or simply from sitting in a hot car. On a sunny 80° day, the temperature inside your parked car (even with the windows partly rolled down) will climb well above 100° in just minutes, putting your pet in danger of permanent damage to the brain and internal organs, and even death.

Recognizing the danger signs

Symptoms of heatstroke may include some or all of the following: frenzied barking; a vacant expression or wild-eyed stare; rapid or heavy panting; rapid pulse; dizziness or weakness; vomiting or diarrhea; deep red or purple tongue and gums (the normal color is light pink, except in breeds where the gums and tongue are naturally black); twitching, convulsions or coma.

Use a rectal thermometer to check your dog's body temperature. Normal body temperature is 100° to 101°—but it can rise to 106° or more with heatstroke.

First aid for heatstroke

First, get your dog out of the sun. Then cover him with towels soaked in cool water, or pour cool water over him every few minutes. *Do not* immerse him in ice water or apply ice directly to his skin, but an ice pack is okay if wrapped in a towel.

Give him a small amount of cool water to drink, or let him lick ice cubes or a bit of plain vanilla ice cream. (Remember—no chocolate!) As soon as his body temperature begins to come down, take him to the nearest veterinarian for follow-up care.

Keeping your pet safe in cold weather

Many dogs, Ginger included, love outdoor activities in snowy weather. But don't assume that your dog is as safe and comfortable as you are in your insulated boots and down-filled clothing. Wintertime hazards include hypothermia, frostbite, and irritation from road salt and other de-icing chemicals.

After playing outside, wash off any remaining ice or road salt, and towel him dry. Then give him a well-deserved rest in a warm place—but not too close to a fireplace or space heater. If he's really chilled, he could burn himself before even realizing it.

Watch out for hypothermia

Smaller or older dogs are most likely to suffer from hypothermia. However, exposure to the cold *when wet* can be extremely hazardous for any dog, especially if immersed in icy water for even a few minutes. When your pet starts to lag behind you instead of bounding ahead, that's the signal to get him back indoors and warmed up. If he becomes listless, ignores your calls and just wants to lie down in the snow, you've stayed out too long—get him indoors!

Dry him off and help to restore his circulation by rubbing vigorously with a towel. Wrap him in a warm blanket, and offer warm (not hot) water if he's willing to drink. If his body temperature drops below 98.5° take him to a veterinarian *immediately*.

Treating for frostbite

When the weather turns windy, check frequently to see if your dog's feet, ears, and tail are getting pale or numb. If so, bring him indoors right away. Massage the affected areas *very gently* with your hands or a soft dry towel to encourage circulation—rough handling can bruise damaged tissues. Soak frostbitten paws or tail in lukewarm (90°) water to gradually restore circulation. Keep him warm and see, or at least *call*, a veterinarian for follow-up care.

6: If Your Dog Gets Lost

You've heard the saying "if you carry an umbrella, it won't rain." Hopefully, being prepared in case your dog gets lost will work the same way for you. And it will remind you of how important—and easy—it is to *prevent* losing him.

The basic prevention measures (you've seen all these before) include:

- Make sure your dog is *always* wearing his collar with ID tags attached. (See p. 11 for information on proper travel tags.)

- Put his leash on *before* letting him out of your car or motel room—and hold onto the other end!

- *Never* leave him alone and unrestrained—he should be in his travel crate or at least inside your car, with adequate ventilation and shade.

That said, if by some fluke you and your dog do get separated, don't panic. Your cool-headed actions now, plus a few advance preparations, will maximize your chances of finding him as quickly as possible.

Preparing a Lost Dog poster

Your first advance effort should be in creating a master lost-and-found poster, complete with your dog's photo and detailed description. Feel free to copy the fill-in-the-blanks poster on the following pages and use it to create your own poster.

First, write a brief description of your pet. Include his name, age, breed, sex (and if neutered or spayed), coat and eye color, height (at top of head or ears when standing), weight, and any special characteristics, such as a crooked tail or a limp.

Second, dig out a close-up photo of your pet, or take a new one right now. It should clearly show his color, any distinctive markings and his relative size. Photograph your dog standing beside a person or a car, for example. Have copies made of this photo that you can attach to multiple copies of your completed lost-and-found poster when needed.

List your home phone number—for leaving a message—and if possible, also list another number that will be answered by a live person who can receive

LOST DOG

Name: **Ginger** Breed: **German Shepherd** Age: **5 yrs**

Sex: **Spayed female** Ht: **30"** Wt: **60 lbs**

Collar: **red nylon** Eye color: **golden brown**

Coat color & length: **tan w/black markings, short straight hair**

ID tags: **Yamhill County license #3617, Rabies tag #03756**

Distinctive markings or behaviors:

Very friendly with people but standoffish with other dogs.

Black ears, muzzle, back and tip of tail

Last seen at:

east end of Memorial Park, near corner of Market & First Sts, approx 3:15 p.m. Monday 8-1-98

Owners: **Linn & Barbara Whitaker**

Staying at: **The Adobe Resort**

Address: **1555 Hwy 101, Yachats OR**

Local Phone: **541-547-3200**

Dates at this location: **Aug 1-3, 1998**

Home Phone: **503-625-3001 after 8-3-98**

(Call collect or leave message and we will reimburse you.)

REWARD!

LOST DOG

Name:

Sex:

Collar:

Coat color & length:

ID tags:

Distinctive markings
or behaviors:

Breed:

Ht:

Eye color:

Age:

Wt:

Attach photo of
your dog here

Last seen at:

Owner's name:

Staying at:

Address:

Local Phone:

Dates at this location:

Home Phone :

(Call collect or leave message and owner will reimburse you)

REWARD!

and relay messages for you. Of course, if you have a mobile phone that works in the area you're visiting, list that number as well. Leave blank spaces for the name, address and phone number of your motel. You'll add that information when you actually need to use the poster.

Store the master poster and photos with your dog's other travel papers, which I recommend keeping in a plastic bag inside his first aid kit. Also tuck in a broad tipped marking pen.

Searching for your lost dog

As soon as you realize your pet is missing, begin searching the immediate area in an ever-widening spiral pattern. Keep calling your dog's name—if he's within the sound of your voice, *he'll* find *you*.

It's important to search *on foot*, not in your car, for several reasons. First, if you're walking, your dog is more likely to catch your scent and come back to you. Second, when you're cruising along in the car, your pet may hear you call him, but by the time he runs to that location, you could be a block—or a mile—away, missing him altogether.

Try to enlist the aid of other people in your search, and offer them a reward. Children are especially good at finding lost animals.

When to call for reinforcements

If you've already searched for an hour or two without finding your dog, it's time to move on to public announcements. Place calls to the police or county sheriff's office, the dog pound or humane society, and the local veterinary clinics to see if they've already found your pet.

Remember to tell everyone if your dog has been implanted with an identification microchip (see p. 13 for more information).

Leave your local phone number with everyone you speak to, and check back periodically. Also ask if there is a local radio or TV station that broadcasts lost pet announcements as a public service. (Then after you find your dog, be sure to let all these folks know, so they don't continue to put out the alert!)

Putting up Lost Dog posters

If you've already checked with local authorities and still haven't found your dog, you'll need to start posting Lost Dog notices around the area. That way, when someone does find him, they'll know how to contact you.

Get out your master poster and fill in the name, address, and phone number of the place where you're staying. Then take it to the local quick print shop, or any other store with a copy machine available, and run off multiple copies for posting around town. Use white or light-colored background sheets—neon yellow is especially eye-catching from a distance and still light enough to be readable.

Attach a photo of your pet to each poster copy. If you only have one original photo, you could attach it to your master poster and then make multiple *color copies* at the quick print shop.

Beginning at the location where your dog was last seen and spiraling outward again, start putting up your posters wherever people congregate:

- On bulletin boards in parks, shopping malls, or in front of convenience stores

- In store windows—ask for permission first!

- At bus stops or parking lot entrances

- On street signs or light posts, especially where cars are likely to be stopping or moving slowly

- Near schools or churches

Since the motel's phone number appears on each poster, notify them of your situation right away. If you can, have a family member stay by the phone in your room in case that all-important "found dog" call comes in while you're out searching. If not, see if the folks at the front desk can take messages for you.

Keep checking back at the place where your dog disappeared, in case he returns there. By the end of the day, he will be increasingly hungry, thirsty, and anxious about being separated from you. Leave a handful of his food there, along with something that has your scent on it, such as a dirty sock. Finding this sign of you during the night may encourage him to stay there until you come back in the morning.

Stay in the local area as long as possible—even if you don't find your pet right away, he may reappear after another day or two. For example, a compassionate resident may take him in overnight, then deliver him to the local dog pound or animal shelter the next day.

When you do have to leave town, be sure to leave your home phone number with everyone—motel management, police, dog pound, local veterinarians—along with instructions to call you *collect.*

And of course, check your home phone often for messages. If your dog is picked up and traced by his license number, rabies tag number or microchip ID, you'll be contacted at your *permanent* address and phone number, so keep those lines of communication open as well.

May your dog never get lost

Your pet is a beloved member of your family, and I sincerely hope you never lose him. Please, spend just a minute or two reviewing the simple steps at the beginning of this chapter to prevent losing him in the first place.

Happy travels to you and your dog from Ginger and myself— and Spike too!

Part II
Reference Section
Hotels—Motels—B & B Listings
Emergency Clinics
Useful Books
Listings Index
Topics Index

A: Where to Stay in Oregon With Your Dog

This directory is alphabetized by city, then business name. If you know the name but not the city, you can look it up in the Listings Index on pp. 255–279. All the hotels, motels and bed & breakfast inns listed here allow dogs in some but not necessarily all rooms. Always call ahead to reserve one of their dog-friendly units. Also be aware that many establishments accept dogs "at the manager's discretion only," meaning they reserve the right to refuse overly dirty, large or out-of-control pets.

The room rates shown are "before tax" in most cases, and are accurate as of the time each location was contacted prior to the publication of this book. However, as in most industries, all rates are subject to change without notice, so ask for the current prices when you call for reservations.

If you don't see one of your favorite establishments listed here, don't despair. Some folks said that although they do accept dogs, they didn't wish to "go public" with that information, and therefore requested not to be included in this directory. However, most of them also said that they will continue to accept return customers who've stayed there with their dogs in the past.

Deciphering these listings

I've tried to include as much useful information as possible in each listing, especially dog-related tips. As more and more dog-friendly lodgings were discovered, some abbreviations became necessary!

food/drink

R = restaurant on the premises
L = lounge in or attached to the restaurant
B&B= bed & breakfast

free

C = complimentary coffee (sometimes also tea or hot chocolate) in the room or in the lobby
CB = continental breakfast
FB = full breakfast

How each listing is laid out:

name	phone #	# of units
address	toll-free #	price range
city-state-zip	fax #	

kitchen

K =   full kitchen or kitchenette in the room

R =   refrigerator, either included or available upon request for an additional fee

M =   microwave oven, same note as refrigerator

pet fee

$ =   fee shown is for each dog, either per day or for the entire stay, as indicated in individual listing

ref dep = refundable damage deposit; can be in the form of an open credit card charge slip or a check—either of which is then returned at checkout if no damage has occurred

pool (may be seasonal or year round)

in =   indoor or covered

out =   outdoor

htd =   heated

spa/sauna

X =   spa, sauna, or hot tub avail for guest use

extra info

items of further interest to dog owners

food/drink	free	kitchen	pet fee	pool	spa/sauna	extra info
R	C	K	$	in	X	any extra information
&	CB	R	per	out		that would be useful
L	FB	M	day	htd		to dog owners

Oregon cities with dog-friendly accommodations

City	Number	City	Number
Agness	3	Cave Junction	3
Albany	9	Charleston	1
Arlington	1	Chemult	6
Ashland	13	Chiloquin	3
Astoria	5	Christmas Valley	2
Azalea	1	Clackamas	1
Baker City	12	Clatskanie	1
Bandon	9	Cloverdale/	
Beaverton	1	Woods	1
Bend	29	Condon	1
Biggs Junction/		Coos Bay	14
Wasco	2	Coquille	1
Blue River	2	Corvallis	9
Boardman	2	Cottage Grove	5
Brightwood	1	Crescent	2
Brookings	8	Crescent Lake	4
Burns	5	Creswell	1
Camp Sherman	5	Curtin	1
Cannon Beach	10	Dallas	1
Canyonville	2	Depoe Bay	3
Cascade Locks	3	Detroit	2

City	Number	City	Number
Diamond Lake	1	Huntington	2
Elgin	2	Idleyld Park	2
Enterprise	2	Irrigon	1
Eugene	14	Jacksonville	1
Fields	1	John Day	6
Florence	5	Jordan Valley	2
Fort Klamath	1	Joseph	3
Fossil	2	Junction City	1
Garibaldi	3	Klamath Falls	18
Gearhart	2	La Grande	8
Glendale	1	La Pine	8
Gleneden Beach	2	Lake Oswego	3
Glide	1	Lakeside	1
Gold Beach	9	Lakeview	6
Gold Hill	2	Lebanon	2
Government Camp	3	Lincoln City	24
Grande Ronde	1	Madras	7
Grants Pass	22	Manzanita	2
Halfway	3	Maupin	2
Halsey	1	McKenzie Bridge	2
Hammond	1	McMinnville	2
Heppner	1	Medford	21
Hermiston	3	Merlin	2
Hillsboro	4	Merrill	1
Hood River	7	Milton-Freewater	2

93

Oregon cities with dog-friendly accommodations < continued >

City	Number	City	Number
Mitchell	1	Oxbow	1
Molalla	1	Pacific City	2
Monmouth	2	Pendleton	10
Moro	1	Philomath	1
Mt. Hood	1	Phoenix	1
Mt. Vernon	2	Pilot Rock	1
Myrtle Creek	1	Port Orford	4
Myrtle Point	1	Portland	42
Neskowin	1	Prairie City	2
Netarts	1	Prineville	4
Newberg	2	Prospect	2
Newport	14	Rainier	1
North Bend	4	Redmond	3
North Powder	1	Reedsport	8
Nyssa	1	Richland	1
O'Brien	1	Riley	1
Oakland	1	Rockaway Beach	11
Oakridge	4	Roseburg	12
Ontario	12	Rufus	2
Oregon City	1	Salem	12
Otter Rock	1	Sandy	2

City	Number	City	Number
Scappoose	1	Vernonia	1
Seaside	17	Vida	2
Shady Cove	2	Waldport	5
Silverton	1	Wallowa	1
Sisters	5	Warm Springs	1
South Beach	2	Warrenton	2
Spray	1	Welches	1
Springfield	6	Westlake	2
St. Helens	1	Westport	1
Stayton	1	Wheeler	1
Sublimity	1	Wilsonville	6
Summer Lake	2	Winchester Bay	3
Sunriver	1	Winston	2
Sutherlin	2	Wolf Creek	1
Sweet Home	2	Woodburn	2
The Dalles	9	Yachats	8
Tigard	5	Yamhill	1
Tillamook	5	Total	702
Tolovana Park	2		
Trail	2		
Troutdale	3		
Tualatin	1		
Ukiah	1		
Umatilla	3		
Unity	1		

Agness — Albany

Cougar Lane Lodge 04219 Agness Rd Agness, OR 97406	541/247-7233 541/247-4046 (fax)	6 units $40-$60
Lucas Pioneer Ranch & Lodge 3904 Cougar Lane Agness, OR 97406	541/247-7443	12 units $45-$65
Singing Springs Ranch PO Box 68 Agness, OR 97406	541/247-6162	9 units $40-$45
Best Western Pony Soldier Motor Inn 315 Airport Rd SE Albany, OR 97321	541/928-6322 800/634-7669 541/928-8124 (fax)	72 units $73-$90
Brier Rose Inn B & B 206 7th Ave SW Albany, OR 97321	541/926-0345	4 units $59-$89
Budget Inn 2727 Pacific Blvd SE Albany, OR 97321	541/926-4246 541/926-5208 (fax)	47 units $37-$45
City Center Motel 1730 Pacific Blvd SE Albany, OR 97321	541/926-8442	16 units $30-$50
Comfort Inn 251 Airport Rd SE Albany, OR 97321	541/928-0921 541/928-8055 (fax)	50 units $61-$150
Holiday Inn Express 1100 Price Rd Albany, OR 97321	541-928-5050 800/928-5657 541/928-4665 (fax)	78 units $59-$80

A: Where to Stay in Oregon with Your Dog

food/drink	free	kitchen	pet fee	pool	spa/sauna	extra info
R & L		K	$3-5 per day			pet fee varies by size of dog, dogwalking area, service station, convenience store
R		K	$5 per stay			cabins & rooms in lodge, river view, lots of area for walking dogs
R & L	C	K	$5 per day			cabins & rooms, 6-bedroom house also avail, restaurant open May 1–Oct 31
				out		AAA & Senior rates, large dogwalking area, 5 minute walk to open field
B & B	FB		$10 per day			near park for walking dogs, email address: brierrose@skipnet.com
		K	$5 per day			laundry facilities, close to park with pond & picnic area
		K R M	$10 ref dep			refundable pet deposit, area for walking dogs, 3 blocks to public park
	C CB	K		in 24 hr	X	24 hr coffee & microwave in lobby, laundry facilities, area for walking dogs
R & L	CB	K		out	X	laundry facilities, exercise room, area for walking dogs

Albany — Ashland

Motel Orleans	541/926-0170	78 units
1212 Price Rd SE	800/626-1900	$40-$59
Albany, OR 97321	541/967-3283 (fax)	
Star Dust Motel	541/926-4233	30 units
2735 Pacific Blvd SE		$30-$75
Albany, OR 97321	541/926-4233 (fax)	
Valu Inn by Nendels	541/926-1538	60 units
3125 Santiam Hwy SE		$35-$43
Albany, OR 97321	541-928-0576 (fax)	
Village Inn	541/454-2646	34 units
131 Beech St		$42
Arlington, OR 97812	541/454-2377 (fax)	
Ashland Knight's Inn	541/482-5111	40 units
2359 Ashland St	800/547-4566	$51-$62
Ashland, OR 97520		
Ashland Motel	541/482-2561	27 units
1145 Siskiyou Blvd	800/468-8858	$43-$80
Ashland, OR 97520		
Ashland Patterson House	541/482-9171	3 units
639 N Main St	888/482-9171	$80-$110
Ashland, OR 97520		
Best Western Bard's Inn	541/482-0049	92 units
132 N Main St	800/528-1234	$95-$175
Ashland, OR 97520	541/488-3259 (fax)	
Best Western Heritage Inn	541/482-6932	53 units
434 E Valley View Rd	800/528-1234	$87-$130
Ashland, OR 97520	541/482-8905 (fax)	
Cedarwood Inn	541/488-2000	64 units
1801 Siskiyou Blvd	800/547-4141	$39-$58
Ashland, OR 97520	541/482-2000 (fax)	

A: Where to Stay in Oregon with Your Dog

food/drink	free	kitchen	pet fee	pool	spa/sauna	extra info
R & L	C	R M	ref dep	out		senior rates avail, area for walking dogs
		K	$10 ref dep			laundry facilities (coin op)
R		R M		out		seasonal pool, movie rental avail, area for walking dogs
R & L		R	$6 per day			laundry facilities
R & L	C		$6 per day	out	X	area for walking dogs
		K R	$5 per day	out		laundry facilities, area for walking dogs, close to public park
B & B	FB					lg yard, near bike trails, one well-behaved dog only (no puppies)
	C CB	R	$10 per day	out	X	1 block from public park
	CB	K		in htd	X	24 hr pool & spa, small grassy area for walking dogs
	C	K	$6 per day	out in	X	dogs allowed Oct 15–April 15 only, walking paths for exercising dogs

Ashland — Astoria

Flagship Quality Inn	541/488-2330	60 units
2520 Ashland St	800/334-2330	$58-$123
Ashland, OR 97520	541/482-1068 (fax)	
Green Springs Inn	541/482-0614	8 units
11470 Hwy 66		$49-$89
Ashland, OR 97520	541/488-3942 (fax)	
Nightingail's Inn	541/482-7373	3 units
117 North Main	800/460-8037	$110
Ashland, OR 97520		
Rodeway Ashland Valley Inn	541/482-2641	64 units
1193 Siskiyou Blvd	800/547-6414	$72-$88
Ashland, OR 97520	541/488-1656 (fax)	
Super 8 Motel	541/482-8887	67 units
2350 Ashland St	800/800-8000	$54-$77
Ashland, OR 97520	541/482-0914 (fax)	
Vista Motel	541/482-4423	18 units
535 Clover Ln		$36-$48
Ashland, OR 97520		
Windmill's Ashland Hills Inn	541/482-8310	230 units
2525 Ashland St	800/547-4747	$88-$225
Ashland, OR 97520	541/488-1783 (fax)	
Bayshore Motor Inn	503/325-2205	77 units
555 Hamburg Ave	800/621-0641	$60-$95
Astoria, OR 97103	503/325-5550 (fax)	
Crest Motel	503/325-3141	40 units
5366 Leif Erickson Dr	800/421-3141	$53-$83
Astoria, OR 97103	503-325-3141 (fax)	
Lamplighter Motel	503/325-4051	29 units
131 W Marine Dr		$52-$72
Astoria, OR 97103	503/325-4239 (fax)	

A: Where to Stay in Oregon with Your Dog

food/drink	free	kitchen	pet fee	pool	spa/sauna	extra info
	C CB	K R	$6 per day	out		area for walking dogs
R					X	in-room spa, laundry facilities, adjacent to open woods for walking dogs
B & B	FB					dogs allowed at owner's discretion only, area for walking dogs
R & L	C	R M	$6 per day	out	X	dogs allowed in smoking rooms only, area for walking dogs
	C	R	ref dep	out in		laundry facilities, area for walking dogs
	C	R M	$10 ref dep	out		back yard for walking dogs
	C CB	R M		out	X	laundry facilities, area for walking dogs, bicycles avail, group-senior-AAA discounts
	C CB	R M		in	X	free newspaper, laundry facilities, area for walking dogs
	C				X	continental breakfast avail for a small fee, river view, yard for walking dogs
	C	R	$4 per day			area for walking dogs, river view

Astoria — Baker City

Red Lion Inn–Astoria 400 Industry St Astoria, OR 97103	503/325-7373 800/547-8010	124 units $45-$150
Rivershore Motel 59 W Marine Dr Astoria, OR 97103	503/325-2921 800/253-2921 503/325-4193 (fax)	43 units $40-$70
Havenshire B & B 1098 Hogum Creek Rd Azalea, OR 97410	541/837-3511	2 units $60-$65
Baker City Motel & RV Park 880 Elm St Baker City, OR 97814	541/523-6381 800/931-9229	17 units $27-$35
Budget Inn of Baker 134 Bridge St Baker City, OR 97814	541/523-6571 800/932-9220 541/523-9424 (fax)	40 units $30-$40
Eldorado Inn 695 Campbell St Baker City, OR 97814	541/523-6494 800/537-5756 541/523-6494 (fax)	56 units $36-$46
Geiser Grand Hotel 1996 Main St Baker City, OR 97814	541/523-1889 888/434-7374 541/523-3991 (fax)	30 units $85-$175
Grant House B & B 2525 3rd St Baker City, OR 97814	541/523-6685 800/606-7468	3 units $55-$75
Green Gables Motel 2533 10th St Baker City, OR 97814	541/523-5588	12 units $26-$42

A: Where to Stay in Oregon with Your Dog

food/drink	free	kitchen	pet fee	pool	spa/sauna	extra info
R & L		K	$10 per stay			area for walking dogs, river view
		K	$5 per day			small dogs only, river view
B & B	FB	K				2 rooms, 1 w/private bath, on 60 acres, 5 acre parkland surrounded by forest
	C	R M	$3 per day			laundry facilities, river view
	C	R M	$3 per stay			laundry facilities, picnic site, area for walking dogs
		R	$2 per day	in		1/4 mile to public park
R & L			$0-$20 /day			"dog refreshments" served, hospitality bar, spa suites, 1/2 block to river, 4 blks to park
B & B	C FB	R M	$10 ref dep			kitchen privileges, close to public park
	C	K	$5 per day			laundry facilities, area for walking dogs, 10 blocks to river & public park

Baker City — Bandon

Oregon Trail Motel & Restaurant 211 Bridge St Baker City, OR 97814	541/523-5844 800/628-3982 541/523-6593 (fax)	54 units $30-$45
Powder River B & B RR 87 Box 500 Baker City, OR 97814	541/523-7143 800/600/7143	2 units $50-$80
Quality Inn 810 Campbell St Baker City, OR 97814	541/523-2242 800/228-5151 541/523-2242 (fax)	54 units $45-$52
Royal Motor Inn 2205 Broadway St Baker City, OR 97814	541/523-6324 800/547-5827 541/523-6324 (fax)	36 units $35-$52
Trail Motel 2815 10th St Baker City, OR 97814	541/523-4646	4 units $25-$40
Western Motel 3055 10th St Baker City, OR 97814	541/523-3700 800/481-3701	14 units $28-$36
Bandon Beach Motel 1110 11th St SW Bandon, OR 97411	541/347-4430	28 units $55-$95
Bandon Wayside Motel RR 2 BOX 385 Bandon, OR 97411	541/347-3421	10 units $32-$42
Caprice Motel RR 1 Box 530 Bandon, OR 97411	541/347-4494	15 units $34-$65

food/drink	free	kitchen	pet fee	pool	spa/sauna	extra info
R			$3-5 per day	out htd		$3 for small pets, $5 for large pets, area for walking dogs
B & B	C FB	R M				full breakfast (can accommodate special dietary needs), guided fishing trips
	CB	R	$2 per day			microwave in lobby, pool avail 2 blocks away, area for walking dogs
	C CB	R M	$4 per day	out htd		4 blocks to park for walking dogs, weekly & monthly rates available
		K				area for walking dogs, near public swimming pool
	C	R	$5 per day			laundry facilities, area for walking dogs
	C CB	K	$5 per day	in htd		small dogs allowed at mgr's discretion, located 1/2 block from 13-acre national park
	C					picnic & barbecue facilities, area for walking dogs
	C	K				small dog only, laundry facilities, area for walking dog

Bandon — Bend

Driftwood Motel	541/347-9022	20 units
460 Hwy 101	888/374-3893	$35-$80
Bandon, OR 97411	541/347-2045 (fax)	
Harbor View Motel	541/347-4417	59 units
355 2nd St	800/526-0209	$67-$80
Bandon, OR 97411	541/347-3616 (fax)	
Inn at Face Rock	541/347-9441	55 units
3225 Beach Loop Rd	800/638-3092	$49-$229
Bandon, OR 97411	541/347-2532 (fax)	
Lamplighter Motel	541/347-4477	16 units
40 North Ave NE	800/650-8817	$28-$65
Bandon, OR 97411		
Sunset Oceanfront Resort	541/347-2453	57 units
1755 Beach Loop Rd	800/842-2407	$53-$175
Bandon, OR 97411	541/347-3636 (fax)	
Table Rock Motel	541/347-2700	15 units
840 Beach Loop Rd		$30-$90
Bandon, OR 97411		
Greenwood Inn	503/643-7444	250 units
10700 SW Allen Blvd	800/289-1300	$87-$125
Beaverton, OR 97005	503/626-4553 (fax)	
Alpine West Lodge	541/389-0250	17 units
61440 S Hwy 97		$25-$28
Bend, OR 97702		
Bend Cascade Hostel	541/389-3813	7 units
19 SW Century Dr	800/299-3813	$14/ea
Bend, OR 97702		person
Bend Holiday Motel	541/382-4620	25 units
880 SE 3rd St	800/252-0121	$30-$65
Bend, OR 97702		

food/drink	free	kitchen	pet fee	pool	spa/sauna	extra info
	C	K	$5 per day			$10 refundable pet deposit, located near boat basin, area for walking dogs
	C CB	R	$10 per day		x	walking path to Old Town, harbor view
R & L		K R M	$6- $15/ stay		X	laundry facilities, ocean view, area for walking dogs
		K				No pets on furniture or left alone in rooms, area for walking dogs
R & L	C	K R	$5 per day		X	laundry facilities, ocean view, area for walking dogs
		K	$5 per day			ocean view, beach access, please keep dogs away from bird/mammal sanctuary
R & L	C	K R M	$10 per day	out htd	X	exercise room, valet & room service
		K R M				dogs on leash only, two large areas for walking dogs, pens also avail for horses
	C	K R M				dogs allowed at manager's discretion, laundry facilities, shared kitchen privileges
	CB	K R M			X	

Bend

Bend Riverside Motel & Condominiums 1565 NW Hill St Bend, OR 97709	541/389-2363 800/284-2363 541/389-2363 (fax)	200 units $49-$110
Best Western Inn & Suites of Bend 721 NE 3rd St Bend, OR 97701	541/382-1515 800/528-1234 541/382-1515 (fax)	102 units $49-$89
Budget Inn 1300 SE Hwy 97 Bend, OR 97702	541/389-1448	23 units $30-$40
Cascade Lodge 420 SE 3rd St Bend, OR 97702	541/382-2612 800/852-6031 800/852-6031 (fax)	33 units $35-$60
Chalet Motel 510 SE 3rd St Bend, OR 97702	541/382-6124 541-317-4916 (fax)	22 units $30-$55
Cimarron Motor Inn–North 437 NE 3rd St Bend, OR 97701	541/382-7711 800/304-4050 541-385-0989 (fax)	59 units $34-$54
Cimarron Motor Inn–South 201 NE 3rd St Bend, OR 97701	541/382-8282 800/304-4050 541/388-6833 (fax)	59 units $34-79
Comfort Inn 61200 S 3rd St Bend, OR 97702	541/388-2227 800/228-5150 541/388-8820 (fax)	65 units $51-$81
Cultus Lake Resort Hwy 46 Century Dr PO Box 262 Bend, OR 97701	541/389-3230 800/616-3230	23 cabins $52-$89

food/drink	free	kitchen	pet fee	pool	spa/sauna	extra info
	C	K	$5 per day	in	X	pets allowed in smoking units only, river or park view
	CB	R M	$5 per day	out	X	24 hr coffee in lobby, book ahead for nonsmoking pet rooms, area for walking dogs
	C	K M	$5 per day			dogs allowed at manager's discretion only, area for walking dogs
	CB	K	$5 per day	out	X	area for walking dogs
	CB	K	$4 per day			area for walking dogs
R & L	CB	K R M	$5 per day	out		24 hr coffee in lobby, area for walking dogs
R & L	C CB	K R M	$5 per day	out		RV parking, 24 hr coffee in lobby, area for walking dogs
	CB	K		in 24 hr	X	24 hr sauna & Jacuzzi, laundry facilities, area for walking dogs
R		K	$5 per day			open May 16–Oct 19, lake view, fireplaces, electric heat, modern baths

Bend

Gazebo Bed & Breakfast 21679 Obsidian Ave Bend, OR 97702	541/389-7202	2 units $40-$60
Inn Appropriate 63911 Sunrise Circle Bend, OR 97701	541/388-0047 541/389-3523	1 cottage $95
Motel West 228 NE Irving Ave Bend, OR 97701	541/389-5577 800/282-5577 541/389-5577 (fax)	39 units $36-$52
Mount Bachelor Motel 2359 NE Division St Bend, OR 97701	541/382-6365	19 units $27
Palmer's Motel 645 NE Greenwood Ave Bend, OR 97701	541/382-1197	9 units $30-$45
Pines Lodge, The 61405 S Hwy 97 Bend, OR 97702	541/389-5910 800/500-5910	13 units $39-$89
Red Lion Inn–North 1415 NE 3rd St Bend, OR 97701	541/382-7011 800/733-5466 541/382-7934 (fax)	75 units $64-$115
Red Lion Inn–South 849 NE 3rd St Bend, OR 97701	541/382-8384 800/733-5466 541/382-9180 (fax)	75 units $69-$92
Riverhouse Resort, The 3075 N Hwy 97 Bend, OR 97701	541/389-3111 800/547-3928 541/389-0870 (fax)	220 units $68-$95
Rodeway Inn 3705 N Hwy 97 Bend, OR 97701	541/382-2211 800/507-2211 541/382-2211 (fax)	36 units $30-$85

A: Where to Stay in Oregon with Your Dog

food/drink	free	kitchen	pet fee	pool	spa/sauna	extra info
B & B	FB	R M	$5 per day			dogs at manager's discretion only, quiet country roads for walking dogs
	C	K	ref dep		X	separate cottage, 2 night minimum, area for walking dogs
	C	K				
		R M	$5 per day			$25 nonrefundable deposit, laundry facilities, pet area in back, park across street
R		K R M	$4 per day			nonsmoker's motel
	CB	K	$5 per day			rustic "log cabin" style rooms, all are nonsmoking
R & L				out	X	no dogs alone in room
	C CB			out	X	
R & L	C	K R		out in	X	fireplaces, river view, spa, sauna, in-room spa, area for walking dogs
		R M	$5 per stay	out	X	close to public park

Bend — Biggs Junction

Royal Gateway Motel	541/382-5631	25 units
475 SE 3rd St		$30-$60
Bend, OR 97702	541/317-9107 (fax)	
Shilo Inn–Bend Suites Hotel	541/389-96000	151 units
3105 O.B. Riley Rd	800/222-2244	$75-$165
Bend, OR 97701	541/382-4310 (fax)	
Sleep Inn of Bend	541/330-0050	59 units
600 NE Bellevue	800/627-5337	$49-$69
Bend, OR 97701	541/383-8109 (fax)	
Sonoma Lodge	541/382-4891	17 units
450 SE 3rd St		$39-$59
Bend, OR 97702	541/382-4891 (fax)	
Super 8 Motel	541/388-6888	79 units
1275 SE Hwy 97	800/800-8000	$49-$67
Bend, OR 97702	541/389-9056 (fax)	
Tom Tom Motel	541/382-4734	10 units
3600 N Hwy 97	800/246-3434	$32-$35
Bend, OR 97701		
Westward Ho Motel	541/382-2111	65 units
904 SE 3rd St	800/999-8143	$37-$75
Bend, OR 97702	541/382-3848 (fax)	
Best Western Riviera	541/739-2501	40 units
91484 Biggs-Rufus Hwy	800/528-1234	$52-$85
Biggs Junction/Wasco,	541/739-2091 (fax)	
OR 97065		
Dinty's Motor Inn at	541/739-2596	26 units
Biggs Junction		$38-$68
91581 Biggs-Rufus Hwy	541/739-2232 (fax)	
Biggs Junction/Wasco, OR 97065		

food/drink	free	kitchen	pet fee	pool	spa/sauna	extra info
	C	K R M	$5 per day			pet fee may be waived at manager's discretion, area for walking dogs
R & L	C FB	K R M	$7 per day	out in	X	free breakfast buffet, Deschutes river frontage, fitness center
	C CB	R M	$8 per stay	out	X	large open area for walking dogs, quiet location
	CB	K R M	$3-5 per day			multiple-night discount, no pets alone in rooms
	C CB	R	$25 ref dep	in	X	laundry facilities, Super 8 VIP discounts
R	C	R M	$6-$12/ day			fee varies with dog's size, laundry facilities, remodeled rooms
	C	K R M		in	X	fireplaces
	CB	R	$5 per day	out		dogs allowed at manager's discretion only, open area for walking dogs, close to river
	C	R	$25 ref dep			dogs allowed at manager's discretion, mini-mart & deli

Blue River — Brookings

McKenzie River B & B 55482 Delta Rd Blue River, OR 97413	541/822-8232 888/355-2583	2 units $75-$105
Woodland Cottages 52560 McKenzie Hwy Blue River, OR 97413	541/822-3597	3 cabins $65-$90
Dodge City Inn 1st & Front Sts Boardman, OR 97818	541/481-2451 541/481-3563 (fax)	40 units $39-$65
Nugget Inn 105 Front St SW Boardman, OR 97818	541/481-2375 800/336-4485 541/481-2600 (fax)	51 units $40-$69
Oregon Ark Motel 61716 Hwy 26 Brightwood, OR 97011	503/622-3121 503/622-4881 (fax)	15 units $28-$45
Beaver State Motel 437 Chetco Ave Brookings, OR 97415	541/469-5361	17 units $36-$55
Best Western Beachfront Inn 16008 Boat Basin Rd Brookings, OR 97415	541/469-7779 800/468-4081 541/469-0283 (fax)	78 units $79-$165
Bonn Motel 1216 Chetco Ave Brookings, OR 97415	541/469-2161	37 units $45-$65
Casa Rubio PO Box 397 Brookings, OR 97415	707/487-4313 800/357-6199	4 units $68-$98
Harbor Inn Motel 15991 Hwy 101 S Brookings, OR 97415	541/469-3194 800/469-8444 541/469-0479 (fax)	30 units $45-$72

A: Where to Stay in Oregon with Your Dog

food/drink	free	kitchen	pet fee	pool	spa/sauna	extra info
B & B	FB					can arrange catered lunch or dinner, near hiking trails, golf course & river guides
	C	K				small dogs only, river view, rustic housekeeping cabins
R & L		R M		out		4 blocks from river, public park across street, gift shop & banquet room
R & L	CB	K R M		out		
	C CB	K R	$10 per day			rustic setting on 20 acres with 5 acres of pasture & 5 ponds on property
	C	K	$10 per day			
R & L		K R M	$5 per day	out htd	X	pets allowed in ocean view bldg. only, laundry facilities
R & L	C	K	$3 per day	in htd	X	open area for walking dogs, 1/2 mile to public park
	CB	K				female dog only, oceanfront, free dinner at Rubio's in Brookings w/2-night stay
	C		$5 per day			ocean view in some rooms

Brookings — Camp Sherman

Pacific Sunset Inn	541/469-2141	40 units
1144 Chetco Ave	800/469-2141	$36-$100
Brookings, OR 97415	541/469-7837 (fax)	
Sea Dreamer Inn	541/469-6629	3 units
15167 McVay Ln	800/408-4367	$60-$75
Brookings, OR 97415		
Westward Motel	541/469-7471	32 units
1026 Chetco Ave, PO Box 1079		$55-$95
Brookings, OR 97415		
Best Western Ponderosa Inn	541/573-2047	52 units
577 W Monroe St	800/303-2047	$48-$96
Burns, OR 97720	541/573-3828 (fax)	
Bontemps Motel	541/573-2037	15 units
74 W Monroe St	800/229-1394	$31-$74
Burns, OR 97720	541/573-2577 (fax)	
Orbit Motel	541/573-2034	31 units
Hwy 20 & Hwy 395 North, PO Box 303		$28-$40
Burns, OR 97720	541/573-2601 (fax)	
Royal Inn	541/573-1700	38 units
999 Oregon Ave		$44-$58
Burns, OR 97720	541/573-2331 (fax)	
Silver Spur Motel	541/573-2077	26 units
789 N Broadway Ave	800/400-2077	$34-$44
Burns, OR 97720	541/573-3921 (fax)	
Black Butte Resort Motel	541/595-6514	6 units
& RV Park		$55-$65
25635 SW Forest Svc Rd 1419	541/595-5971 (fax)	
Camp Sherman, OR 97730		

A: Where to Stay in Oregon with Your Dog

food/drink	free	kitchen	pet fee	pool	spa/sauna	extra info
		K	$5 per day			microwave available, AAA & senior rates, area for walking dogs
B & B	FB		ref dep			close to walking trails, other dogs on premises so call for advance reservations
	C		$5 per stay			dogs under 10 lbs only, area for walking dogs, 3/4 mile to beach access
R & L	CB	R avail	$5 per stay	out htd		microwave avail in lobby, area for walking dogs
	C	K R M				BBQ avail, laundry facilities, free passes to theater next door, area for walking dogs
	C	K R M	$2 per day	out		area for walking dogs
	C	R M	ref dep	in	X	$20 refundable pet deposit, laundry facilities, area for walking dogs
	CB	R M	$5 per day		X	health club facilities
	C	K R	$7 per day			laundry facilities, gathering room avail

Camp Sherman—Cannon Beach

Cold Springs Resort & RV Park "On the Metolius River" HCR 1270 Camp Sherman, OR 97730	541/595-6271 541/595-1400 (fax)	2 cabins $88-$103
Lake Creek Lodge Camp Sherman Rd Camp Sherman, OR 97730	541/595-6331 800/797-6331 541/595-1016 (fax)	16 cabins $110-$160
Metolius River Lodges County Rd #700, PO Box 110 Camp Sherman, OR	541/595-6290 800/595-6290 541/595-6290 (fax)	12 units $58-$98
Twin View Resort Star Route Box 2126 Camp Sherman, OR 97730	541/595-6125	6 units $54-$98
Cannon Beach Ecola Cr Lodge 208 5th St Cannon Beach, OR 97110	503/436-2776 800/873-2749 503/436-9550 (fax)	21 units $65-$160
Guest House Motel 1016 S Hemlock Cannon Beach, OR 97110	503/436-0630 800/585-0630	2 units $66-$125
Hallmark Resort—Cannon Beach 1400 S Hemlock St Cannon Beach, OR 97110	503/436-1566 888/448-4449 503/436-0324 (fax)	132 units $69-$425
Haystack Motel 3339 S. Hemlock St Cannon Beach, OR 97110	503/436-1577 800/499-2220 503/436-0749 (fax)	23 units $79-$179
Land's End Motel 263 W. 2nd St Cannon Beach, OR 97110	503/436-2264 800/793-1477	14 units $98-$125

food/drink	free	kitchen	pet fee	pool	spa/sauna	extra info
		K M	$6 per day			fully equipped cabins, BBQ avail, 1+ acre of riverfront lawn for walking dogs
R		K	$8 per day	out		Summer rate (Jun–Sep) includes dinner, studio & 2 or 3 bdrm cabins avail
	CB	K R M	$6 per day			dogs allowed Oct–May only, fireplaces, river view, bdrm units or cabins
		K	$5 per day			adjacent to wooded area for walking dogs
	CB	K	$10 per day			laundry facilities
		K			X	no pets alone in rooms, 1 block to beach, in-room jacuzzi
R & L	C	K R	$8 per day	in	X	in-room spa avail, ocean view, laundry facilities, exercise room
	C	K R	$5 per day	in	X	free newspaper, ocean view, newly refurbished, 1 block to beach, across from state park
	C	K R M	$8 per day		X	dogs allowed Sep 15–Jun 1 only, ocean view, laundry facilities

Cannon Beach—Cascade Locks

McBee Motel Cottages	503/436-2569	10 units
888 S. Hemlock St		$39-$105
Cannon Beach, OR 97110	503/436-1396 (fax)	
Quiet Cannon Lodgings	503/436-1405	2 units
372 N. Spruce St		$85-$95
Cannon Beach, OR 97110		
Sandcastle Condominiums	503/436-1577	8 units
3507 S Hemlock St	800/547-6100	$189-$209
Cannon Beach, OR 97110	503/436-9116 (fax)	
Surfsand Resort	503/436-2274	82 units
Oceanfront & Gower Sts	800/547-6100	$119-$299
Cannon Beach, OR 97110	503/436-9116 (fax)	
Tasha's Garden–Vacation	503/436-9610	1 unit
Rental for People with Pets		$70
PO Box 1156	503/436-9609 (fax)	
Cannon Beach, OR 97110		
Leisure Inn	541/839-4278	37 units
554 SW Pine		$37-$55
Canyonville, OR 97417		
Valley View Motel	541/839-4550	11 units
1926 Stanton Park Rd		$39-$60
Canyonville, OR 97417		
Best Western Columbia	541/374-8777	63 units
River Inn	800/595-7108	$79-$124
735 Wanapa St, PO Box 580	541/374-2279 (fax)	
Cascade Locks, OR 97014		
Bridge of the Gods Motel	541/374-8628	15 units
& RV Park		$40-$65
630 Wanapa St, PO Box 98	541/374-2217 (fax)	
Cascade Locks, OR 97014		

food/drink	free	kitchen	pet fee	pool	spa/sauna	extra info
	C	K	$5 per day			1 or 2 pets only; check-in at Cannon Beach Hotel Lodgings
		K	$5 per stay			ocean & creek views, fireplaces
		K	$5 per day	in	X	1/2 block to public park, 1 block to beach
R & L	C	K R M	$5 per day	in	X	free newspaper, ocean view, in-room spa, laundry, email: surfsand@transport.com
	C	K				fully equipped cottage, yard for walking dogs, close to beach
	C	K		out htd		near Seven Feathers Casino, seasonal pool May 15–Sep 30
	C		$3 per stay			next to Umpqua River, large area for dogs to play, dog groomer on premises
	C CB	R M	$10 per stay	in	X	area for walking dogs, river view, 1 mile to public park
		K				dogs under 30 lbs only, river view, laundry facilities

Cascade Locks — Chemult

Scenic Winds Motel 10 SE Wanapa St, PO Box 344 Cascade Locks, OR 97014	541/374-8390	9 cabins $40-$69
Country Hills Resort 7901 Caves Hwy Cave Junction, OR 97523	541/592-3406 800/997-8464	11 units $40-$60
Junction Inn 406 S Redwood Hwy PO Box 429 Cave Junction, OR 97523	541/592-3106 800/592-4INN 541/592-2112 (fax)	60 units $50-$62
Out 'n' About Tree House Resort 300 Page Creek Rd Cave Junction, OR 97523	541/592-2208 800/200-5484	4 units $75-$125
Captain John's Motel 8061 Kingfisher Dr Charleston, OR 97420	541/888-4041 541/888-6563 (fax)	46 units $40-$70
Chemult Motel PO Box 117 Chemult, OR 97731	541/365-2228 541/365-2228 (fax)	16 units $38-$44
Crater Lake Motel PO Box 190 Chemult, OR 97731	541/365-2241 541/365-2241 (fax)	20 units $27-$85
Dawson House Lodge 1st St and Hwy 97 Chemult, OR 97731	541/365-2232	8 units $35-$85
Holiday Village Motel PO Box 95 Hwy 97 Chemult, OR 97731	541/365-2394	8 cabins $28-$55

A: Where to Stay in Oregon with Your Dog

food/drink	free	kitchen	pet fee	pool	spa/sauna	extra info
		K R M	$5 per stay			river or mtn views, area for walking dogs, 1/2 mile to Pacific Crest trail
	CB	K	$5 per day			laundry facilities, camp store, campground with tent & RV sites
R			$25 per stay	out		area for walking dogs, 10% off dinner in the restaurant, free coffee with breakfast, laundry facilities
	CB	K R M	$10 ref dep	out		riverfront area for walking dogs, horseback riding, www.treesort@magic.net
	C CB	K R M	$5 per stay			
R	C CB	R M				free VCR & movies, shuttle to Amtrak station
	C	K R M				
	CB					no pets alone in room, close to Amtrak station
	C	K				A-frame cabins with knotty pine interiors

Chemult — Cloverdale

Singing Pines Ranch Motel US Hwy 97 Chemult, OR 97731	541/365-9909 541/365-2228 (fax)	8 units $30-$40
Whispering Pines Motel HC 30 Box 140 Chemult, OR 97731	541/365-2259	10 units $30-$40
Melita's Motel & Cafe 39500 Hwy 97 N Chiloquin, OR 97624	541/783-2437 541/783-3028 (fax)	13 units $30-$50
Sportsman Motel Box 27627 Hwy 97 North Chiloquin, OR 97624	541/783-2867	10 units $31-$65
Spring Creek Ranch Motel 47600 Hwy 97 N Chiloquin, OR 97624	541/783-2775	10 units $22-$32
Christmas Valley Desert Inn PO Box 148 Christmas Valley, OR 97641	541/576-2262	16 units $23-$38
Lakeside Terrace Motel PO Box 767 Christmas Valley, OR 97641	541/576-2309 541/576-2309 (fax)	10 units $28-$49
Clackamas Inn 16010 SE 82nd Dr Clackamas, OR 97015	503/650-5340 800/874-6560 503/657-7221 (fax)	44 units $56-$93
Northwoods Inn 945 E Columbia River Hwy Clatskanie, OR 97016	503/728-4311	31 units $31-$52
Raines Resort 33555 Ferry St Cloverdale/Woods, OR 97112	503/965-6371	7 units $30-$65

food/drink	free	kitchen	pet fee	pool	spa/sauna	extra info
		K R M				fireplaces
R	C	K R M				laundry facilities, sled dog races held nearby during January & February
R & L			fee varies			pet fee may be required, laundry facilities, RV park
	C	K R	$5 per day			rooms–cabins–house, senior discount, area for walking dogs, 1 mile to Klamath Lake
	C	K				fireplaces, creek frontage
	C	K R				lots of open area for walking dogs
R		R M	ref dep			private patios, airport shuttle, dogwalking area, RV park
	C CB	R M	$5 per day	out		24 hr coffee in lobby, laundry facilities
		K R M				daily maid service, car wash
	C	K	$5 per day			dogs allowed Nov–Jul only, fully furnished cabins, dock, RV park on Nestucca River

Condon — Coos Bay

Condon Motel	541/384-2181	18 units
276 N Washington St		$34-$40
Condon, OR 97823	541/384-2182 (fax)	
Bay Park Motel	541/267-3743	10 units
655 Newport Ave (Hwy 101 S)		$27-$45
Coos Bay, OR 97420		
Bayshore Motel	541/267-4138	34 units
1685 N Bayshore Dr		$32-$70
Coos Bay, OR 97420		
Best Western Holiday Motel	541/269-5111	77 units
411 N Bayshore Dr	800/228-8655	$71-$150
Coos Bay, OR 97420	541/269-5111 (fax)	
Coos Bay Manor	541/269-1224	5 rooms
955 S 5th St	800/269-1224	$75-$95
Coos Bay, OR 97420	541/269-1224 (fax)	
Edgewater Inn	541/267-0423	81 units
275 E Johnson Ave	800/233-0423	$65-$105
Coos Bay, OR 97420	541/267-4343 (fax)	
Motel 6	541/267-7171	94 units
1445 N Bayshore DR	800/4-MOTEL-6	$33-$45
Coos Bay, OR 97420	541/267-4618 (fax)	
Old Tower House B & B	541/888-6058	5 units
476 Newmark Ave		$80
Coos Bay, OR 97420	541/888-6058 (fax)	
Plainview Motel & RV Park	541/888-5166	10 units
2760 Cape Arago Hwy	800/962-2815	$38-$75
Coos Bay, OR 97420		
Red Lion Inn–Coos Bay	541/267-4141	143 units
1313 N. Bayshore Dr	800/547-8010	$75-$110
Coos Bay, OR 97420	541/267-2884 (fax)	

food/drink	free	kitchen	pet fee	pool	spa/sauna	extra info
	C	K R M	$5 per day			area for walking dogs, near city park & swimming pool, 20 miles to fossil beds
	C	K	$50 ref dep			area for walking dogs, weekly rates avail
	C		$5 per day			area for walking dogs, 1 mile from casino, harbor view, close to beach access
	CB	K R	$10 per day	in	X	exercise room, laundry facilities, area for walking dogs, access to boardwalk
B & B	C FB		$10 per stay			dogs on leash at all times, residential area for walking dogs, near park & boardwalk
	C CB	K R M	$8 per day	in	X	bay view
	C	K			X	jacuzzi in some rooms, laundry facilities, area for walking dogs
B & B	C FB					dogs allowed in 1 unit, close to the water, open area for walking dogs
	C	K	$5 per day			laundry facilities, crab rings & cooker avail for guest use
R & L	C	R M		out		laundry facilities, area for walking dogs

Coos Bay — Corvallis

Sea Psalm Motel 1250 Cape Arago Hwy PO Box 3415 Coos Bay, OR 97420	541/888-9053	8 units $30-$35
Southsider Motel 1005 S Broadway Coos Bay, OR 97420	541/267-2438	11 units $28-$43
Terrace Motel 1109 S 1st St Coos Bay, OR 97420	541/269-5061 541/269-5061 (fax)	15 units $30-$60
This Olde House B & B 202 Alder Ave Coos Bay, OR 97420	541267-5224	4 units $65-$90
Timber Lodge Motel 1001 N Bayshore Dr PO Box 578 Coos Bay, OR 97420	541/267-7066 800/782-7592 541/269-2527 (fax)	53 units $39-$102
Myrtle Lane Motel 787 N Central Blvd Coquille, OR 97423	541/396-2102 541/396-2911 (fax)	25 units $32-$48
Ashwood B & B, The 2940 NW Ashwood Dr Corvallis, OR 97330	541/757-9772 800/306-5136 541/758-1202 (fax)	3 units $60-$70
Corvallis Budget Inn 1480 SW 3rd St Corvallis, OR 97333	541/752-8756 541/752-8756 (fax)	24 units $35-$65
Econo Lodge 345 NW 2nd St Corvallis, OR 97330	541/752-9601 800/553-2666 541/752-0042 (fax)	61 units $38-$46

food/drink	free	kitchen	pet fee	pool	spa/sauna	extra info
		R				country setting, large yard for walking dogs
	C					small dogs only, no dogs alone in rooms, area for walking dogs
	C	K				area for walking dogs
B & B	C FB					small dog only, reservations required, complimentary wine, tea, coffee
R & L	C	R M	$5 per stay			area for walking dogs, in-room spa
	C	K R M	$4 per day			picnic area
B & B	FB		$5 per stay			close to university & fairgrounds, health club use
		K R M				
	C	R M	$5 per day			in-room spa, river view

Corvallis — Cottage Grove

Jason Inn 800 NW 9th St Corvallis, OR 97330	541/753-7326 800/346-3291 541/753-7326 (fax)	51 units $36-$48
Motel Orleans 935 NW Garfield Ave Corvallis, OR 97330	541/758-9125 800/626-1900 541/758-0544 (fax)	61 units $49-$62
Shanico Inn 1113 NW 9th St Corvallis, OR 97330	541/754-7474 800/432-1233 541/754-2437 (fax)	76 units $46-$56
Super 8 Motel 407 NW 2nd Corvallis, OR 97330	541/758-8088 800/800-8000 541/758-8267 (fax)	101 units $53-$73
Towne House Motor Inn 350 SW 4th St Corvallis, OR 97333	541/753-4496 800/898-4496 541/753-4496 (fax)	100 units $35-$55
Travel Inn 1562 SW 3rd St Corvallis, OR 97333	541/752-5917	15 units $28-$42
Best Western Village Green 725 Row River Rd Cottage Grove, OR 97424	541/942-2491 800/343-7666 541/942-2386 (fax)	96 units $59-$115
City Center Motel 737 Hwy 99 S Cottage Grove, OR 97424	541/942-8322 541/942-8322 (fax)	15 units $30-$35
Cottage Grove Comfort Inn 845 Gateway Blvd Cottage Grove, OR 97424	541/942-9747 800/944-0287 541/942-8841 (fax)	58 units $54-$100
Holiday Inn Express 1601 Gateway Blvd Cottage Grove, OR 97424	541/942-1000 800/HOLIDAY 541/942-1077 (fax)	41 units $73-$99

food/drink	free	kitchen	pet fee	pool	spa/sauna	extra info
R & L			$4 per day	out		1/2 mile from OSU
	C	R M	ref dep		X	laundry facilities, AAA & senior rates
R	C CB	R M	$5 per day	out		24 hr coffee avail in lobby, room service, AAA rates
	C CB		ref dep	in	X	laundry facilities, Super 8 VIP discounts
R & L	C	K	$6 per day			laundry facilities
		K R		out		
R & L	C	R	$5 per day	out htd	X	tennis courts, golf, RV park, jogging trails nearby
	C	R M	$5 per day			laundry facilities, lake view
	CB		$5-$10/ day	out	X	24 hr coffee in lobby, free newspaper
	C CB	R M	$10 per day	in htd	X	laundry facilities, area for walking dogs, exercise room

Cottage Grove — Curtin

Relax Inn 1030 Hwy 99 N Cottage Grove, OR 97424	541/942-5132	24 units $25-$30
Crescent Motel Hwy 97 & Jones St, PO Box 192 Crescent, OR 97733	541/433-2550	8 units $32-$43
Woodsman Country Lodge Hwy 97 Crescent, OR 97733	541/433-2710 541/433-2917 (fax)	15 units $33-$69
Crescent Creek Cottages & RV Park Hwy 58 Milepost 71 PO Box 7 Crescent Lake, OR 97425	541/433-2324 541/433-2624 (fax)	5 cabins $40-$65
Odell Lake Resort Hwy 58 Milepost 67 E. Exit PO Box 72 Crescent Lake, OR 97425	541/433-2540	19 units $60-$130
Shelter Cove Resort Hwy 58, W. Odell Lake Rd Crescent Lake, OR 97733	541/433-2548	8 cabins $65-$135
Willamette Pass Inn Hwy 58 Milepost 69 Crescent Lake, OR 97733	541/433-2211 800/301-2218 541/433-2855 (fax)	12 units $58-$88
Motel Orleans 345 E Oregon Ave Creswell, OR 97426	541/895-3341 800/626-1900 541/895-3926 (fax)	70 units $38-$43
Stardust Motel 455 Bear Creek Rd, PO Box 80 Curtin, OR 97428	541/942-5706	18 units $25-$35

A: Where to Stay in Oregon with Your Dog

food/drink	free	kitchen	pet fee	pool	spa/sauna	extra info
		K	$5 per day			laundry facilities, lake view, area for walking dogs
	C	R M				free coffee at restaurant across street, river & woods nearby for walking dogs
		K R	$5 per day			fireplace, private patio, in-room spa
		K	$5 per stay			creekside cabins, BBQ pits, RV park, mini-mart
R		K	$5 per day			1 dog only, lakeside cabins
		K				lakeside cabins, great fishing lake
	C CB	K	$15 per stay		X	VCR & movies avail, laundry facilities, large area for dogs to roam
R & L	C		ref dep	out		small dogs only
		K	$5 per day			area for walking dogs

133

Dallas — Enterprise

Riverside Motel	503/623-8163	23 units
517 Main St		$48-$68
Dallas, OR 97338	503/623-8269 (fax)	
Inn at Arch Rock	541/765-2560	12 units
70 NW Sunset St, PO Box 157		$80-$85
Depoe Bay, OR 97341		
Trollers Lodge	541/765-2287	12 units
355 SW Hwy 101 PO Box 800	800/472-9335	$55-$79
Depoe Bay, OR 97341	541/765-3287 (fax)	
Whale Inn at Depoe Bay	541/765-2789	11 units
416 Hwy 101 North, PO Box 414		$60-$85
Depoe Bay, OR 97341	541/765-2754 (fax)	
All Seasons Motel	503/854-3421	15 units
130 Breitenbush Rd, PO Box 565		$40-$80
Detroit, OR 97342		
Detroit Motel	503/854-3344	10 units
75 Detroit Ave, PO Box 4521		$30-$65
Detroit, OR 97342		
Diamond Lake Resort	541/793-3333	93 units
HC 30 Box 1	800/733-7593	$70-$115
Diamond Lake, OR 97731	541/793-3309 (fax)	
Elgin City Centre Motel	541/437-2441	14 units
51 S 7th Ave, PO Box 207		$43-$45
Elgin, OR 97827		
Minam Motel	541/437-4475	8 units
Hwy 82 in Minam, PO Box 369		$26-$47
Elgin, OR 97827		
Ponderosa Motel	541/426-3186	25 units
102 SE Greenwood		$48-$47
Enterprise, OR 97828	541/426-8068 (fax)	

food/drink	free	kitchen	pet fee	pool	spa/sauna	extra info
		K R M	$5 per day			river view
	C CB	K R M	$10 per day			small dogs only, views of ocean & Spouting Horn, beach access in summer
	C	K R M	$5 per day			dogs under 15 lbs only, area for walking dogs, ocean view
	C	R	$5 per day			well mannered dogs only, towels & scoopers provided, trails nearby, dogsitting avail
		K R				dogs allowed in smoking rooms only, lake view, near marina
		K				lots of open area for walking dogs
R & L		K	$5 per day			rooms & cabins, boat & bike rentals, email address: snowrick@aol.com
		K R	$5 per day			small dogs only, laundry facilities, email address: frkunz@oregontrail.net
		K				riverfront area for walking dogs
	C	R	$5 per day			open credit card required for pet, no pets alone in rooms

Enterprise — Eugene

Wilderness Inn Motel	541/426-4535	29 units
301 W. North St	800/965-1205	$48-$80
Enterprise, OR 97828	541/426-0128 (fax)	
Best Western New Oregon	541/683-3669	128 units
Motel, 1655 Franklin Blvd	800/528-1234	$58-$78
Eugene, OR 97403	541/484-5556 (fax)	
Boon's Red Carpet Motel	541/345-0579	24 units
1055 W 6th Ave		$30-$60
Eugene, OR 97402		
Budget Host Motor Inn	541/342-7273	77 units
1190 W 6th Ave	800-554-9822	$45-$75
Eugene, OR 97402		
Campus Inn	541/343-3376	60 units
390 E Broadway	800/888-6313	$46-$70
Eugene, OR 97401	541/343-3376 (fax)	
Country Squire Inn	541/484-2000	105 units
33100 Van Duyn Rd		$33-$100
Eugene, OR 97401	541/484-2431 (fax)	
Eugene Hilton Hotel	541/342-2000	270 units
66 E 6th Ave	800/937-6660	$110-$160
Eugene, OR 97401	541/302-6600 (fax)	
Motel 6 Eugene	541/687-2395	59 units
3690 Glenwood Dr	800/4-MOTEL-6	$38-$50
Eugene, OR 97403	541/687-6828 (fax)	
Quality Inn	541/342-1243	102 units
2121 Franklin Blvd	800/456-6487	$55-$95
Eugene, OR 97403	541/343-3474 (fax)	
Ramada Inn	541/342-5181	148 units
225 Coburg Rd	800/917-5500	$58-$68
Eugene, OR 97401	541/342-5164 (fax)	

food/drink	free	kitchen	pet fee	pool	spa/sauna	extra info
	C	R M	$5 per day		X	open credit card required for pet, no pets alone in rooms
R & L			$25 ref dep	in	X	river view, year-round sports facilities, laundry facilities
		K	$0-5 per day			pet fee varies with dog's size, open area for walking dogs
		R M	$5 per day			area for walking dogs
	C CB	R	ref dep			24 hr coffee in lobby, area for walking dogs
R & L	C	K R M	$0-$10/ day			laundry facilities, large area for walking dogs, pet fee varies
R & L		R M	$25 per stay	out in		laundry service, exercise, room, AAA & senior rates, area for walking dogs
	C					no dogs alone in rooms, area for walking dogs, 1-1/2 miles from Prefontaine Trail
R & L	C CB	R M		out	X	dogs allowed for 1 night in smoking rooms only, 24 hr coffee in lobby
R & L	C CB	R M	$15 per stay	in	X	children's game area, walking trails & public park 2 blocks away

Eugene — Florence

Red Lion Inn–Eugene 205 Coburg Rd Eugene, OR 97401	541/342-5201 800/RED-LION 541/485-2314 (fax)	137 units $69-$100
Sixty-Six Motel 755 E Broadway Eugene, OR 97401	541/342-5041	66 units $29-$41
Travelodge Eugene 1859 Franklin Blvd Eugene, OR 97403	541/342-6383 800/444-6383 541/342-6383 (fax)	60 units $61-$85
Truck 'n' Travel Motel 32910 Van Duyn Rd Eugene, OR 97401	541/485-2137 541/683-2301 (fax)	21 units $35-$48
Valley River Inn 1000 Valley River Way Eugene, OR 97401	541/687-0123 800/543-8266 541/687-0289 (fax)	257 units $145-$190
Fields General Store & Motel HC 77 Box 1 Fields, OR 97710	541/495-2275	4 units $25-$80
Money Saver Motel 170 Hwy 101 Florence, OR 97439	541/997-7131	40 units $32-$48
Ocean Breeze Motel 85165 Hwy 101 S Florence, OR 97439	541/997-2642 800/753-2642	10 units $50-$65
Park Motel 85034 Hwy 101 Florence, OR 97439	541/997-2634 800/392-0441	17 units $34-$79
Silver Sands Motel 1449 Hwy 101 Florence, OR 97439	541/997-3459	50 units $42-$92

A: Where to Stay in Oregon with Your Dog

food/drink	free	kitchen	pet fee	pool	spa/sauna	extra info
R & L	C	R		out	X	health club, courtyard for walking dogs
			$25 ref dep			near university & hospital
R	C CB	R M			X	dogs allowed in smoking rooms only
			$10 per day			dogs allowed in 4 rooms, open field for walking dogs, laundry facilities
R & L				out	X	bike path, river view, exercise room
R						open area for walking dogs, single or double rooms, also group unit w/5 beds, 2 baths
	C		$5 per day			refundable deposit & damage contract, located 1 block from Old Town
	C	K R M	$3 per stay			picnic area, large yard for walking dogs
R		K R M	$5 per day			6-acre area for walking dogs, separate chalet available
	C	K	$5 per day	out		dog walking area

Florence — Glendale

Villa West Motel 901 Hwy 101, PO Box 1236 Florence, OR 97439	541/997-3457	22 units $36-$68
Wilson's Cottages 57997 Hwy 62, PO Box 488 Fort Klamath, OR 97626	541/381-2209	10 units $32-$68
Bridge Creek Flora Inn 828 Main St Fossil, OR 97830	541/763-2355 541/763-2039	5 units $60-$75
Fossil Motel & Trailer Park 105 First St Fossil, OR 97830	541/763-4075	10 units $22-$35
Bayshore Inn 227 Garibaldi Ave Garibaldi, OR 97118	503/322-2552 503/322-2581 (fax)	22 units $59-$106
Harbor View Inn & RV Park 302 S. 7th St, PO Box 257 Garibaldi, OR 97118	503/322-3251	20 units $43-$58
Tilla Bay Motel 805 Garibaldi, PO Box 130 Garibaldi, OR 97118	503/322-3405	11 units $39
Gearhart-By-The-Sea Resort 1157 N. Marion Ave Gearhart, OR 97138	503/738-8331 800/547-0115 503/738-0881 (fax)	80 units $119-$184
Windjammer Motel 4253 Hwy 101 N Gearhart, OR 97138	503/738-3250 800/479-5191	24 units $45-$125
Mt. Reuben Inn 150 Rattlesnake Rd Glendale, OR 97442	541/832-2653 541/832-2501	2 units $80

A: Where to Stay in Oregon with Your Dog

food/drink	free	kitchen	pet fee	pool	spa/sauna	extra info
	C		$5 per stay			pets under 20 lbs only, area for walking dogs
		K				2 & 3 bdrm cottages, full kitchens & baths, next to federal land for walking dogs
	FB					laundry facilities, fenced yard, near parks, museums & historic downtown area
	C	K R M				housebroken dogs only, no barking, creekside walking area, city park next door
	C	K R M	$7 per stay			laundry facilities
		R M	$3 per stay			bay view, firepit & picnic patio, large area for walking dogs
		K				laundry facilities, close to boat dock, small area for walking dogs
	C	K	$10 per day	in htd	X	AAA & senior rates, fully equipped condominiums ocean view
	C	K	$5 per day			no pets alone in room, quiet location, area for walking dogs
B & B					X	handcrafted log guesthouse, private bath, hot tub, lots of area for walking dogs

Gleneden — Gold Beach

Beachcombers Haven	541/764-2252	6 units
7045 NW Glen Ave	800/428-5533	$125-$165
PO Box 275	541/764-4094 (fax)	
Gleneden Beach, OR 97388		
Salishan Lodge	541/764-3685	205 units
7760 Hwy 101 N	800/452-2300	$189-$269
Gleneden Beach, OR 97388		
Steelhead Run B & B	541/496-0563	5 units
23049 N. Umpqua Hwy	800/348-0563	$75
Glide, OR 97443	541/496-3200 (fax)	
City Center Motel	541/247-6675	21 units
94200 Harlow St, PO Box 1339		$40-$80
Gold Beach, OR 97444		
Drift In Motel	541/247-4547	23 units
94250 N Port Dr	800/424-3833	$50-$64
Gold Beach, OR 97444		
Inn at Gold Beach	541/247-6606	41 units
29171 Ellensburg	800/503-0833	$55-$95
Gold Beach, OR 97444	541/247-7046 (fax)	
Ireland's Rustic Lodges	541/247-7718	40 units
29330 S Ellensburg Ave		$52
Gold Beach, OR 97444	541/247-0225 (fax)	
Jot's Resort	541/247-6676	140 units
94360 Wedderburn Loop	800/367-5687	$85-$295
PO Box J		
Gold Beach, OR 97444		
Motel 6 Gold Beach	541/247-4533	50 units
94433 Jerry's Flat Rd	800/759-4533	$30-$70
Gold Beach, OR 97444	541/247-0467 (fax)	

A: Where to Stay in Oregon with Your Dog

food/drink	free	kitchen	pet fee	pool	spa/sauna	extra info
		K	$100 ref dep			oceanfront houses & condominiums, linen service, hot tubs
R & L			$15 per day	in	X	exercise room
B & B	FB	K	$10 per day			well-trained dogs allowed in 1 unit with $100 deposit, riverfront, swimming access
			$10 per day			
	C	K	$5 per day			miniature golf course, area for walking dogs, walking distance to jet boat rides
	C	K	$5 per day			beach access, ocean view, trail behind motel for walking dogs
	C		$5 per day			pets allowed in 8 cabins, ocean view, beach access, yard for walking dogs
R & L	C	K	$10 per day	out in	X	large area for walking dogs, river view, laundry facilities
	C	K			X	trail for walking dogs, river view w/access nearby, laundry facilities

Gold Beach — Grande Ronde

Oregon Trail Lodge 29855 Ellensburg, PO Box 721 Gold Beach, OR 97444	541/247-6030	16 units $38-$65
Shore Cliff by the Sea 29346 Ellensburg Gold Beach, OR 97444	541/247-7091 541/247-7170 (fax)	40 units $60-$72
Western Village Motel 29399 S Ellensburg Ave PO Box 793 Gold Beach, OR 97444	541/247-6611	27 units $50-$80
Flycaster Motel 1356 Rogue River Hwy Gold Hill, OR 97525	541/855-7178	5 units $30
Lazy Acres Motel & RV Park 1550 2nd Ave Gold Hill, OR 97525	541/855-7000	6 units $30-$38
Mount Hood Inn 87450 E. Gov't Camp Loop Government Camp	503/272-3205 800/443-7777 503/272-3307 (fax)	56 units $125-$155
Thunderhead Lodge Condos 87577 Gov't Camp Loop PO Box 129 Government Camp, OR 97028	503/272-3368 800/859-8493 503/272-3368 (fax)	10 units $89-$292
Trillium Lake Basin Cabins 32798 E. Mineral Creek Dr Government Camp, OR 97028	503/297-5993 or 503/272-0151	2 cabins $60-$175
Granny Franny's Farm B & B Grande Ronde, OR 97347	503/879-5002 800/553-9002 (code 61)	2 units $65

A: Where to Stay in Oregon with Your Dog

food/drink	free	kitchen	pet fee	pool	spa/sauna	extra info
	C	K				area for walking dogs
	C		$5 per day			ocean view, beach access
	C	K R M				ocean view, beach access, dogwalking area, outside hose to rinse off sand, etc.
		R M				riverfront, natural area for walking dogs
		K	$1.50 per day			area for walking dogs, river frontage, laundry facilities
	CB	R M	$5 per stay		X	ski lockers, indoor ski tune-up area, indoor parking, laundry facilities
		K R M	$25-$50 dep	out htd		refundable pet deposit, rec room, lots of walking trails, ski right out the back door!
		K				2 & 3 bdrm rustic cabins, ski in 1-1/2 miles x-country to reach cabins, 1 mile to lake
B & B	FB					dog allowed at owner's discretion, resident dog, 3.8 miles to Spirit Mtn Casino

Grants Pass

Best Western Grants Pass Inn	541/476-1117	84 units
111 NE Agness Ave	800/553-ROOM	$71-$127
Grants Pass, OR 97526	541/479-4315 (fax)	
Best Western Inn at the Rogue	541/582-2200	54 units
8959 Rogue River Hwy	800/238-0700	$70-$89
Grants Pass, OR 97527	541/582-1415 (fax)	
Bunny's Motel	541/476-7243	11 units
707 NE 6th St		$35-$40
Grants Pass, OR 97526		
City Center Motel	541/476-6134	21 units
741 NE 6th St		$29-$38
Grants Pass, OR 97526		
Crest Motel	541/479-0720	10 units
1203 NE 6th St		$20-$30
Grants Pass, OR 97526		
Flamingo Inn	541/476-6601	33 units
728 NW 6th St		$25-$40
Grants Pass, OR 97526	541/476-8501 (fax)	
Golden Inn Motel	541/479-6611	60 units
1950 NW Vine St		$49-$54
Grants Pass, OR 97526	541/479-0273 (fax)	
Hawks Inn Motel	541/479-4057	18 units
1464 NW 6th St		$30-$45
Grants Pass, OR 97526		
Ivy House, The	541/474-7363	4 units
139 SW "I" St		$55-$65
Grants Pass, OR 97526		
Knights Inn Motel	541/479-5595	32 units
104 SE 7th St	800/826-6835	$40-$45
Grants Pass, OR 97526	541/479-5256 (fax)	

146

A: Where to Stay in Oregon with Your Dog

food/drink	free	kitchen	pet fee	pool	spa/sauna	extra info
R & L	C	K	$5 per day	out	X	dogs allowed in smoking rooms only, area for walking dogs, laundry facilities
R & L	CB		$10 per stay	out	X	small dogs only, laundry facilities, riverside area for walking dogs
		K	$3 per day			area for walking dogs, close to public park
		K	$5 per day			dogs under 20 lbs only, area for walking dogs
		K	$3-$5 per day			area for walking dogs, close to public park & riverside
		K	$3-$5 per day	out		dog walking area, close to downtown shops, 5 minute walk to public park
	CB	R M	$4 per day	out		area for walking dogs, public parks nearby, laundry facilities
	C		$2 per day	out		adjacent to open field for walking dogs, close to public park
B & B	C FB				X	large yard for walking dogs, close to public park & shops, lunch also served (extra fee)
	C	K	$3 per day			area for walking dogs, laundry facilities, close to riverside park & stores

147

Grants Pass

Motel Orleans	541/479-8301	61 units
1889 NE 6th St	800/626-1900	$46-$63
Grants Pass, OR 97526	541/955-9721 (fax)	
Paradise Resort	541/479-4333	16 units
7000 Monument Dr		$90-$125
Grants Pass, OR 97526	541/479-0218 (fax)	
Redwood Motel	541/476-0878	26 units
815 NE 6th St		$55-$70
Grants Pass, OR 97526	541/476-1032 (fax)	
Regal Lodge Motel	541/479-3305	30 units
1400 NW 6th St		$35-$40
Grants Pass, OR 97526		
Riverside Inn Resort	541/476-6873	174 units
& Conference Ctr	800/334-4567	$65-$275
971 SE 6th St	541/474-9848 (fax)	
Grants Pass, OR 97526		
Rod & Reel Motel	541/582-1516	8 units
7875 Rogue River Hwy	800/516-5557	$40-$75
Grants Pass, OR 97527		
Rogue River Inn	541/582-1120	21 units
6285 Rogue River Hwy		$45-$79
Grants Pass, OR 97527	541/582-4419 (fax)	
Rogue Valley Motel	541/582-3762	7 units
7799 Rogue River Hwy		$49-$79
Grants Pass, OR 97527		
Royal Vue Motor Hotel	541/479-5381	60 units
110 NE Morgan Ln	800-452-1452	$44-$68
Grants Pass, OR 97526	541/479-5381 (fax)	

A: Where to Stay in Oregon with Your Dog

food/drink	free	kitchen	pet fee	pool	spa/sauna	extra info
	C	R M	ref dep	out		AAA & senior rates, laundry facilities
	CB		$10 per day	out	X	pitch-n-putt golf, fish pond, 360 acres for walking dogs, recreation barn w/games
	C CB	K R M	$10 per stay	out	X	designated dog walking area, laundry facilities, 1 mile to Riverside Park
	C		$2 per day			area for walking dogs, 2 miles to Riverside Park
R & L	C	K R M	$15 per stay	out	X	complimentary dog treats, adjacent to public park, www.riverside-inn.com
	C	K R M	ref dep		X	river frontage & woods for walking dogs, picnic tables, BBQ pits
	C	K	$7-$10/ stay	out		large area near river for walking dogs, laundry facilities
	C	K	$5 per day	out htd		small dogs only, next to field & riverside area for walking dogs, dock
R & L	C	R		out	X	area for walking dogs, close to public park, toll-free from outside OR: 800/547-7555

Grants Pass — Heppner

Shilo Inn Grants Pass	541/479-8391	70 units
1880 NW 6th ST	800/222-2244	$59-$79
Grants Pass, OR 97526	541/474-7344 (fax)	
Super 8 Motel	541/474-0888	79 units
1949 NE 7th St	800/800-8000	$44-$68
Grants Pass, OR 97526	541/474-3358 (fax)	
Thriftlodge	541/476-7793	35 units
748 SE 7th St	800/525-9055	$40-$50
Grants Pass, OR 97526	541/479-4812 (fax)	
Clear Creek Farm B & B Inn	541/742-2238	5 units
Rt 1 Box 138	800/742-4992	$60-$66
Halfway, OR 97834	541/742-5175 (fax)	
Halfway Motel	541/742-5722	31 units
170 S Main St, PO Box 740		$35-$70
Halfway, OR 97834		
Pine Valley Lodge	541/742-2027	7 units
163 N Main St, PO Box 912		$65-$140
Halfway, OR 97834		
Pioneer Villa Truck Plaza	541/369-2801	60 units
33180 Hwy 228, I-5 Exit 216		$35-$45
Halsey, OR 97348	541/369-2810 (fax)	
South Jetty Inn	503/861-2500	9 units
984 Pacific Dr, PO Box 151		$50-$65
Hammond, OR 97121		
Northwestern Motel &	541/676-9167	20 units
RV Park	888/851-8436	$35-$50
389 N Main, PO Box 703		
Heppner, OR 97836		

food/drink	free	kitchen	pet fee	pool	spa/sauna	extra info
	C CB	R M	$7 per day	out	X	sauna, steam room, free USA Today newspaper
	C		ref dep	in	X	area for walking dogs. laundry facilities
	C	R M	ref dep	out		2 blocks to public park, near shops & jet boat dock
B & B	FB	R	$25 ref dep		X	rooms & cabins, BBQ, trout ponds, buffalo, pony ride, www.neoregon.com/ccgg
	C	K				dogs allowed in older wing only (no air conditioning)
R & L	C FB	K R M	$10 per stay			room fee includes breakfast, area for walking dogs, close to public park
R & L				out	X	area for walking dogs, mini-mart & service station, restaurant open 24 hrs
		K				area for walking dogs, no dogs alone in room, walking distance to ocean & bay
	C	R M	$5 per stay			near open field for walking dogs, indoor public pool 2 blocks away, museum, library

Hermiston — Hood River

Sands Motel 835 N 1st St Hermiston, OR 97838	541/567-5516 888/5679521 541/567-5516 (fax)	39 units $36-$52
Sunset Motel 425 N 1st Pl Hermiston, OR 97838	541/567-5583 541/567-5583#40 (fax)	34 units $32-$39
Way Inn, The 635 S Hwy 395 Hermiston, OR 97838	541/567-5561 888/564-8767	30 units $32-$48
Best Western Hallmark Inn 3500 NE Cornell Rd Hillsboro, OR 97124	503/648-3500 800/448-4449 503/640-2789 (fax)	123 units $89-$125
Hillsboro Candlewood Hotel 3133 NE Shute Rd Hillsboro, OR 97123	503/681-2121 800/946-6200 503/693-7189 (fax)	126 units $96-$116
Residence Inn by Marriott– Portland West 18855 NW Tanasbourne Dr Hillsboro, OR 97124	503/531-3200 800/331-3131 503/645-1581 (fax)	122 units $112-$168
Townhouse Motel 432 SE Baseline St Hillsboro, OR 97123	503/648-3168	32 units $43-$54
Beryl House B & B 4079 Barrett Dr Hood River, OR 97031	541/386-5567	4 units $65-$75
Best Western Hood River Inn 1108 E Marina Way Hood River, OR 97031	541/386-2200 800/828-7873 541/386-8905 (fax)	149 units $80-$105

A: Where to Stay in Oregon with Your Dog

food/drink	free	kitchen	pet fee	pool	spa/sauna	extra info
R & L	C	K R M	$5 per day	out		large area for walking dogs, close to laundromat-shops- pet grooming & supplies
	C	K				area for walking dogs
	C	R M	$2 per day	out		area for walking dogs, close to public park
R & L	C CB	R M	$5 per day	out	X	laundry facilities, open area for walking dogs, 1 mile to park & walking paths
		K	$10 per day		X	nonrefundable $75 pet fee, next to park for walking dog, free 24 hr laundry facilities
	CB	K	$10 per day	out		laundry facilities, designated area for walking dogs, close to walking paths
		R	$5 ref dep			small dogs only, open area for walking dogs
B & B	FB					well- behaved dogs only, rural area for walking dogs, email: berylhouse@aol.com
R & L	C	R M	$12 per day	out	X	area for walking dogs, near marina & public park, laundry facilities

Hood River — Idleyld Park

Columbia Gorge Hotel 4000 Westcliff Dr Hood River, OR 97031	541/386-5566 800/345-1921 541/387-5414 (fax)	40 units $150-$270
Hood River Hotel 102 Oak Ave Hood River, OR 97031	541/386-1900 800/386-1859 541/386-6090 (fax)	41 units $59-$145
Lone Pine Motel 2429 Cascade Ave Hood River, OR 97031	541/386-2601	6 units $25-$60
Meredith Gorge Motel 4300 Westcliff Dr Hood River, OR 97031	541/386-1515	21 units $36-$46
Vagabond Lodge 4070 Westcliff Dr Hood River, OR 97031	541/386-2992 541/386-3317 (fax)	43 units $42-$79
Farewell Bend Motor Inn 5945 Hwy 30 Huntington, OR 97907	541/869-2211 541/869-2015 (fax)	42 units $39-$50
Wayne's Highway Service 190 W Washington St PO Box 264 Huntington, OR 97907	541/869-2224	7 units $25
Idleyld Park Lodge 23834 N Umpqua Hwy PO Box 347 Idleyld Park, OR 97447	541/496-0088	4 units $45-$65
North Umpqua Resort 23855 N Umpqua Hwy, PO Box 177 Idleyld Park, OR 97447	541/496-0149	7 units $29-$55

food/drink	free	kitchen	pet fee	pool	spa/sauna	extra info
R & L	C					"World Famous Farm Breakfast"® included, area for walking dogs
R & L	CB	K	$15 per day		X	river view, exercise room, close to riverfront area for walking dogs
		K R M				open field for walking dogs, close to public park
	C	K				area for walking dogs, close to public park, river view
	C	K				river view, playground, area for walking dogs, close to public park
R & L	C					river view, area for walking dogs, close to state park, senior & trucker discounts
		K				cabins with kitchenettes, open lot for walking dogs, close to public parks
R	C FB					pool tables in community room, area for walking dogs, hiking trails, close to river
	C	K				motel rooms & a cabin, riverfront location, fishing, swimming, bike path

Irrigon — Jordan Valley

Weary Traveler's Motel Hwy 730 & 1st St, PO Box 698 Irrigon, OR 97844	541/922-2681	9 units $30-$45
Stage Lodge, The 830 N. 5th St, PO Box 1316 Jacksonville, OR 97530	541/899-3953 800/253-8254 541/899-7556 (fax)	27 units $69-$135
Best Western John Day Inn 315 W Main St John Day, OR 97845	541/575-1700 800/243-2628 541/575-1558 (fax)	39 units $49-$99
Budget 8 Motel 711 W Main St John Day, OR 97845	541/575-2155 541/575-2155 (fax)	14 units $39-$55
Budget Inn 250 E Main St John Day, OR 97845	541/575-2100 800/854-4442 541/575-2100 (fax)	14 units $39-$49
Dreamers Lodge Motel 144 N Canyon Blvd John Day, OR 97845	541/575-0526 800/654-2849 541/575-2733 (fax)	25 units $46-$48
John Day Sunset Inn 390 W Main St John Day, OR 97845	541/575-1462 800/452-4899 541/575-1471 (fax)	43 units $40-$82
Traveler's Motel 755 S Canyon Blvd John Day, OR 97845	541/575-2076 541/575-0914 (fax)	17 units $26-$41
Basque Station Motel 801 Main St, PO Box 159 Jordan Valley, OR 97910	541/586-2244 541/586-2448 (fax)	16 units $40-$50
Sahara Motel & Service 607 Main St (Hwy 95) Jordan Valley, OR 97910	541/586-2500 800/828-4432 541/586-2519 (fax)	22 units $32-$54

A: Where to Stay in Oregon with Your Dog

food/drink	free	kitchen	pet fee	pool	spa/sauna	extra info
R & L		K R M				dogs allowed at manager's discretion, weekly rates avail close to park–marina–shops
	C CB		$10 per day			spa suites, area for walking dogs, close to veterinarian & dog groomer
	C	R M	$3.50 per day	in	X	area for walking dogs, 4 blks to public park, laundry facilities, exercise room
	C	R M	$2 per day			dogs in smoking rooms only, swimming pool nearby, open lot for walking dogs
	C	R M	$3 per day			dogs allowed in smoking rooms only, close to public park
	C	K				area for walking dogs, close to public park
R & L	C	R M	$3.50 per day	in	X	dogs allowed in smoking rooms only, area for walking dogs, close to public park
	C	R M				mini-mart, laundry facilities, small area for walking dogs
						area for walking dogs, 4 blocks to public park
	C		$3 per day			close to public park

Joseph — Klamath Falls

Indian Lodge Motel 201 S Main St Joseph, OR 97846	541/432-2651 541/432-4949 (fax)	16 units $37-$55
Mountain View Motel & RV Park 83450 Joseph Hwy Joseph, OR 97846	541/432-2982	9 units $32-$58
Stein's Cabins 84681 Ponderosa Lane Joseph, OR 97846	541/432-2391	8 units $65-$175
Guest House Motel, The 1335 Ivy St (Hwy 99) Junction City, OR 97448	541/998-6524 800/835-5170 541/998-8932 (fax)	22 units $44-$54
A-1 Budget Motel 3844 Hwy 97 N Klamath Falls, OR 97601	541/884-8104	32 units $38-$50
Best Western Klamath Inn 4061 S 6th St Klamath Falls, OR 97603	541/882-1200 800/528-1234 541/882-2729 (fax)	52 units $55-$75
Cimarron Motor Inn 3060 S 6th St Klamath Falls, OR 97603	541/882-4601 800/742-2648 541/882-6690 (fax)	163 units $48-$56
Econo Lodge 75 Main St Klamath Falls, OR 97601	541/884-7735 800/553-2666 541/882-7095 (fax)	52 units $39-$71
Golden West Motel 6402 S 6th St Klamath Falls, OR 97603	541/882-1758 541/885-2955 (fax)	14 units $28-$50

A: Where to Stay in Oregon with Your Dog

food/drink	free	kitchen	pet fee	pool	spa/sauna	extra info
	C	R	$5-$10/ stay			area for walking dogs, 2 blocks to public park, 1 mile to lake
		K	$5 per stay			area near stream for walking dogs
		K	$5 per day			cabins–cottages–houses, area for walking dogs, grocery store, close to lake
	C					can request ground floor unit, area for walking dogs, close to public park
	C CB	K		in		area for walking dogs, lake view from some rooms, laundry facilities
	CB	R M		in		walking trails adjacent to motel, discounts avail for AAA, AARP & truckers
	C CB	R	$5 per stay	out		area for walking dogs, laundry facilities, close to public park
	C CB		$10 per stay			across street from public park & lake
	C	K R M	$5 1-3 days			mobile home also avail, large yard for walking dogs, weekly rates with $35 pet fee

Klamath Falls

High Chaparral Motel 5440 Hwy 97 N Klamath Falls, OR 97601	541/882-4675	33 units $27-$89
Hill View Motel 5543 S 6th St Klamath Falls, OR 97603	541/883-7771 541/883-7771 (fax)	16 units $35-$50
La Vista Motor Lodge 3939 Hwy 97 N Klamath Falls, OR 97601	541/882-8844 541/882-8434 (fax)	24 units $36-$46
Lake of the Woods Resort 950 Harriman Rt Klamath Falls, OR 97601	541/949-8300 541/949-8220 (fax)	8 units $55-$80
Maverick Motel 1220 Main St Klamath Falls, OR 97601	541/882-6688 800/404-6690 541/885-4095 (fax)	49 units $32-$36
Motel 6 5136 S 6th St Klamath Falls, OR 97603	541/884-2110 800/4-MOTEL-6 541/882-3384 (fax)	61 units $38-$50
New Wheel Inn Motel 5805 S 6th St Klamath Falls, OR 97603	541/850-6066 541/850-6068 (fax)	16 units $32-$69
Olympic Lodge 3006 Green Springs Dr Klamath Falls, OR 97601	541/883-8800	32 units $32-$47
Quality Inn 100 Main St Klamath Falls, OR 97601	541/882-4666 800/732-2025 541/883-8795 (fax)	80 units $63-$96

A: Where to Stay in Oregon with Your Dog

food/drink	free	kitchen	pet fee	pool	spa/sauna	extra info
	C	K	$5 per day			guest kitchen avail, area for walking dogs, close to public park, 1 mile to lake
	C	R M				small dogs only, area for walking dogs
	CB			out	X	yard area for walking dogs, laundry facilities, river view
R & L		K				lakefront, lots of trails for walking dogs, boat rental, tackle shop, RV parking
	C CB		$5 per stay	out		seasonal swimming pool, small grassy area for walking dogs
R	C			out htd		laundry facilities, area for walking dogs, close to public park
	C	K R M				dogs allowed at manager's discretion only, 1-1/2 blocks to public park & trails
	CB		$10 ref dep	out		area for walking dogs, river view, horse corrals avail
R & L	C CB	R M	$50 ref dep	out	X	Close to Lake Ewauna & Veterans Park for walking dogs, laundry facilities

Klamath Falls — La Grande

Shilo Inn–Klamath Falls Suites Hotel 2500 Almond St Klamath Falls, OR 97601	541/885-7980 800/222-2244 541/885-7959 (fax)	143 units $89-$129
Super 8 Motel 3805 Hwy 97 N Klamath Falls, OR 97601	541/884-8880 800/800-8000 541/884-0235 (fax)	61 units $48-$64
Townhouse Motel 5323 S 6th St Klamath Falls, OR 97603	541/882-0924 541/882-0924 (fax)	18 units $25-$32
Travelodge 11 Main St Klamath Falls, OR 97601	541/882-4494 800/578-7878 541/882-8940 (fax)	36 units $34-$42
Blue Mountain Motel 2313 E Adams La Grande, OR 97850	541/963-4424	10 units $23-$45
Budget Inn 2215 E Adams Ave La Grande, OR 97850	541/963-7116 541/963-2015 (fax)	34 units $32-$49
Greenwell Motel 305 Adams Ave La Grande, OR 97850	541/963-4134 541/963-2691 (fax)	33 units $25-$35
Howard Johnson Inn of La Grande 2612 Island Ave La Grande, OR 97850	541/963-7195 800/IGO-HOJO 541/963-4498 (fax)	146 units $67-$87
Moon Motel 2116 Adams Ave La Grande, OR 97850	541/963-2724	9 units $30-$34

162

A: Where to Stay in Oregon with Your Dog

food/drink	free	kitchen	pet fee	pool	spa/sauna	extra info
R & L	C CB	R M	$7 per day	in	X	free newspaper, 24 hr rec center, laundry facilities, in-room video players
	C		ref dep		X	area for walking dogs, Super 8 VIP discounts
		K				area for walking dogs, close to walking trails, close to 24 hr restaurant, shops
	CB	R M		out		riverfront, across street from public park
		K R M	$5 per day			area for walking dogs
	C CB	K	$5 per day			area for walking dogs, close to public park
	CB			out htd		area for walking dogs, close to public park
	C CB	R		out	X	grassy area for walking dogs, fitness center, AAA & senior discounts
	C	R M	$5 per day			small dogs only, public park across street

La Grande — La Pine

Orchard Motel 2206 E Adams Ave La Grande, OR 97850	541/963-6160	12 units $30-$45
Quail Run Motor Inn 2400 Adams Ave La Grande, OR 97850	541/963-3400 541/963-8516 (fax)	15 units $25-$35
Stardust Lodge 402 Adams Ave La Grande, OR 97850	541/963-4166 541/963-8695 (fax)	32 units $30-$45
Diamond Stone Guest Lodge 16693 Sprague Loop La Pine, OR 97739	541/536-6263 800/600-6263 541/536-9711 (fax)	3 units $75-$150
East Lake Resort PO Box 95 La Pine, OR 97739	541/536-2230	16 cabins $35-$95
Highlander Motel 51511 Hwy 97 La Pine, OR 97739	541/536-2131 541/536-5246 (fax)	9 units $30-$50
Lampliter Motel & RV Park 51526 Hwy 97, PO Box 379 La Pine, OR 97739	541/536-2931	5 units $34
Newberry Station Motel 16515 Reed Rd La Pine, OR 97739	541/536-5130 800/210-8616 541/536-7779 (fax)	40 units $55-$150
Paulina Lake Resort PO Box 7 La Pine, OR 97739	541/536-2240	14 cabins $65-$135
Timbercrest Inn 52560 Hwy 97 La Pine, OR 97739	541/536-1737 541/536-2563 (fax)	21 units $31-$40

food/drink	free	kitchen	pet fee	pool	spa/sauna	extra info
	C CB	K R M	$5 per day			small dogs only, area for walking dogs, close to public park, pet porter available
	CB	K R M	$3-$4 per day			small dogs only, area for walking dogs, picnic area
	C CB	R M	$5 per day	out		close to public park for walking dogs
B & B	FB		$10 per day		X	walking distance to river for swimming & walking dogs, www.diamondstone.com
		K	$5 per day			18 miles off Hwy 97, 1 dog per cabin only, in heart of Newberry Nat'l Monument
	C	K				area for walking dogs, 3 blocks to public park, trailer spaces, service station
	C	R M	$10 ref dep			area for walking dogs, laundry facilities
	C CB	K R M	$25 ref dep	in	X	area for walking dogs
R		K R M	$7 per day			open May–October, 1 dog per cabin only, dogs must be on leash at all times
	C	K				bring your own kitchen equipment, trails & open area for walking dogs

La Pine — Lakeview

West View Motel 51371 Hwy 97, PO Box 497 La Pine, OR 97739	541/536-2115 800/440-2115	9 units $32-$50
Best Western Sherwood Inn 15700 SW Upper Boones Ferry Rd Lake Oswego, OR 97035	503/620-2980 503/639-9010 (fax)	101 units $54-$74
Crowne Plaza Hotel 14811 SW Kruse Oaks Blvd Lake Oswego, OR 97035	503/624-8400 800/227-6963 503/684-8324 (fax)	161 units $125-$300
Residence Inn by the Marriott—Portland South 15200 SW Bangy Rd Lake Oswego, OR 97035	503/684-2603 800/331-3131 503/620-6712 (fax)	112 units $110-$175
Lakeshore Lodge 290 S 8th, PO Box B Lakeside, OR 97449	541/759-3161 541/759-3161 (fax)	20 units $44-$76
Best Western Skyline Motor Lodge 414 North G St Lakeview, OR 97630	541/947-2194 800/528-1234 541/947-3100 (fax)	38 units $60-$66
Budget Inn–Lakeview 411 North F St Lakeview, OR 97630	541/947-2201	14 units $34-$40
Hunter's Hot Springs Resort Hwy 395, PO Box 1189 Lakeview, OR 97630	541/947-2125 800/979-4350 541/947-5496 (fax)	30 units $40-$75
Interstate 8 Motel 354 North K St Lakeview, OR 97630	541/947-3341	32 units $34-$38

A: Where to Stay in Oregon with Your Dog

food/drink	free	kitchen	pet fee	pool	spa/sauna	extra info
	C	K				dogs allowed in smoking rooms only, area for walking dogs
R & L	C		$10 per day	in	X	quiet area for walking dogs, no pets alone in room
R & L	C	R M		in	X	complimentary beverage in lounge, exercise room, spa suites, walking trails
	CB	K	$10 per day	out	X	seasonal pool, fireplaces in all rooms, laundry facilities, area for walking dogs
R & L			$5 per day			lakefront, private balconies & patios, private dock, near marina, walking area
	CB		$10 per day			laundry facilities, area for walking dogs, 4 blocks to public park
R	C CB	K R M		out	X	open areas for walking dogs, close to shops & restaurants
R & L	C CB	K	$10 ref dep	out htd	X	natural hot springs pool, www.huntersresort.com
	CB	R	$20 ref dep			area for walking dogs, laundry facilities next door

Lakeview — Lincoln City

Lakeview Lodge Motel 301 North G St Lakeview, OR 97630	541/947-2181 541/947-2572 (fax)	40 units $40-$64
Rim Rock Motel 727 South F ST Lakeview, OR 97630	541/947-2185 541/947-5184 (fax)	27 units $30-$35
Lesita Motel 1830 S Main St Lebanon, OR 97355	541/258-2434	8 units $36-$46
Shanico Inn 1840 S Main St Lebanon, OR 97355	541/259-2601 541/258-2059 (fax)	40 units $41-$61
Anchor Motel & Lodge 4417 SW Hwy 101 Lincoln City, OR 97367	541/996-3810 800/582-8611	29 units $40-$95
Beachfront Garden Inn & Oceanfront Homes 3313 NW Inlet Ave Lincoln City, OR 97367	541/994-2324 360/694-1601 (fax)	12 units $99-$230
Bel-Aire Motel 2945 NW Hwy 101 Lincoln City, OR 97367	541/994-2984	10 units $34-$54
Best Western Lincoln Sands 535 NW Inlet Ave Lincoln City, OR 97367	541/994-4227 800/445-3234 541/994-2232 (fax)	33 units $169-$219
Blue Heron Landing Motel 4006 West Devils Lake Rd Lincoln City, OR 97367	541/994-4708 541/994-2897 (fax)	8 units $57-$108

food/drink	free	kitchen	pet fee	pool	spa/sauna	extra info
	C	K			X	exercise room, area for walking dogs, 3 blocks to public park
	C	K				area for walking dogs, close to public park
		K	$5 per day			area for walking dogs, close to public park
	C	R M avail				small dogs only, area for walking dogs
	C	K				dogs under 10 lbs only, area for walking dogs, beach access nearby, group rates
	C	K R M	$7.50 per day			2 inns, 3 homes, oceanfront with easy beach access, pet relief areas, VCRs, kitchens
			$5 per day			area for walking dogs, 5 blocks from beach
	C CB	K	$10 per day	out htd	X	dogs under 10 lbs only & at mgr's discretion, easy beach access, VCR, hair dryer
	C	K R	$6 per stay			small dogs only, no dogs alone in room, natural areas nearby for walking dogs

Lincoln City

City Center Motel 1014 NE Hwy 101 Lincoln City, OR 97367	541/994-2612 541/994-2612 (fax)	15 units $32-$120
Coho Inn 1635 NW Harbor Ave Lincoln City, OR 97367	541/994-3684 800/848-7006 541/994-6244 (fax)	50 units $79-$104
Edgecliff Motel 3733 SW Hwy 101 Lincoln City, OR 97367	541/996-2055	28 units $50-$125
Enchanted Cottage B & B 4507 SW Coast Lincoln City, OR 97367	541/996-4101 541/996-2682 (fax)	3 units $100-$125
Ester Lee Motel 3803 SW Hwy 101 Lincoln City, OR 97367	541/996-3606 888-996-3606	53 units $60-$120
Hide-a-Way Oceanfront Motel 810 SW 10th St Lincoln City, OR 97367	541/994-8874 541/994-8874 (fax)	6 units $70-$125
Inlet Garden B & B 646 NW Inlet Lincoln City, OR 97367	541/994-7932 888/996-2026	3 units $99-$129
Overlook Motel 3521 SW Anchor Dr Lincoln City, OR 97367	541/996-3300 541/996-8984 (fax)	8 units $69-$156
Pacific Rest B & B 1611 NE 11th St Lincoln City, OR 97367	541/994-2337 888/405-7378	2 rooms $75-$85
Rodeway Inn on the Bay 861 SW 51st St Lincoln City, OR 97367	541/996-3996 800/843-4940 541/994-7554 (fax)	40 units $50-$135

Handwritten margin notes: Rosie · Oregoncoastinn.com · Coast Inn · 888-994-7932

food/drink	free	kitchen	pet fee	pool	spa/sauna	extra info
	C	K R	$5 per day			dogs under 20 lbs only, area for walking dogs
	C	K	$6 per day		X	1 dog under 25 lbs only, ocean view, area for walking dogs, close to beach access
	C CB	K	$5 per day			small dogs only & advance permission required, ocean view, beach access
B & B	FB					private entrance, yard for walking dogs, view of ocean from deck, near harbor seals
	C	K	$5 per day			ocean view, beach access
	C	K M	$5 per day			ocean view, beach access, microwave popcorn & VCR in all rooms, special pet gifts
B & B	FB		$50 ref dep			beach access across street
		K	$3 per day			free newspaper, great ocean view, beach access by car or by stairway
B & B	FB		$15 per stay			small dogs only, private bath & deck, ocean view, area for walking dogs
	CB	K	$5 per stay			in-room jacuzzi, bay or ocean view, beach access

Lincoln City

Sailor Jack's Hidden Cove	541/994-3696	40 units
1035 NW Harbor Ave	888HEAVEHO	$77-$119
Lincoln City, OR 97367	541/994-4121 (fax)	
Sea Echo Motel	541/994-2575	12 units
3510 NE Hwy 101		$38-$60
Lincoln City, OR 97367		
Sea Horse Oceanfront	541/994-2101	55 units
Lodging	800/662-2101	$60-$189
2039 NW Harbor Dr	541/994-8016 (fax)	
Lincoln City, OR 97367		
Seagull Beach-Front Motel	541/994-2948	25 units
1511 NW Harbor Ave	800/422-0219	$70-$180
Lincoln City, OR 97367	541/996-2238 (fax)	
Shilo Inn Oceanfront Resort	541/994-3655	247 units
1501 NW 40th Pl	800/222-2244	$49-$229
Lincoln City, OR 97367	541/994-2199 (fax)	
Shoreline Properties	541/994-7028	multiple
1433-B NW 15th	888/996-2026	(call for
Lincoln City, OR 97367	541/996-3630 (fax) prices)	
Surftides Beach Resort	541/994-2191	123 units
2945 NW Jetty Ave	800/452-2159	$52-$95
Lincoln City, OR 97367	541/994-2727 (fax)	
Westshore Oceanfront Motel	541/996-2001	19 units
3127 SW Anchor Ave	800/621-3187	$74-$130
Lincoln City, OR 97367	541/994-5927 (fax)	
Whistling Winds Motel	541/994-6155	16 units
3264 NW Jetty Ave		$45-$85
Lincoln City, OR 97367		

food/drink	free	kitchen	pet fee	pool	spa/sauna	extra info
	C	K R M	$5 per day		X	"softest beds on the coast," ocean view, beach access, sundeck, quiet cove
			$2 per stay			special "guest dog yard," 3 blocks from beach, close to the casino
	C	K	$5 per day	in	X	ocean view, beach access, area for walking dogs
	C	K M	$5-$25/ stay		X	dogs allowed at manager's discretion, fee based on size, ocean view, beach access
R & L	C	K R M	$7 per day	in	X	laundry facilities, free USA Today newspaper, ocean view
			$50 ref dep			multiple vacation rentals, call for details
R & L		K	$6 per day	in	X	dogs under 20 lbs only, no dogs alone in room, ocean view, laundry facilities
	C	K	$5 per day			ocean view, beach access, area for walking dogs
	C	K M	$10 per stay		X	in-room jacuzzis, area for walking dogs, less than 1/2 block from beach

Madras — Manzanita

Best Western Rama Inn—Madras 12 SW 4th St Madras, OR 97741	541/475-6141 888/RAMA INN 541/475-2982 (fax)	46 units $47-$90
Budget Inn 133 NE 5th St Madras, OR 97741	541/475-3831 541/475-1060 (fax)	30 units $35-$60
Hoffy's Motel 600 North Hwy 26 PO Box 547 Madras, OR 97741	541/475-4633 800/227-6865 541/475-7872 (fax)	99 units $38-$125
Juniper Motel 414 N Hwy 26 Madras, OR 97741	541/475-6186 800/244-1399	22 units $30-$52
Relax Inn Motel 797 SW Hwy 97 Madras, OR 97741	541/475-2117	11 units $32-$37
Royal Dutch Motel 1101 SW Hwy 97 Madras, OR 97741	541/475-2281	10 units $28-$44
Sonny's Motel & Restaurant 1539 SW Hwy 97 Madras, OR 97741	541/475-7217 800/624-6137 541/475-6547 (fax)	44 units $45-$99
San Dune Motel 428 Dorcas Lane Manzanita, OR 97130	503/368-5163 888/368-5163 503/368-5168 (fax)	16 units $55-$105
Sunset Surf Motel 248 Ocean Rd Manzanita, OR 97130	503/368-5224 800/243-8035	41 units $55-$120

174

A: Where to Stay in Oregon with Your Dog

food/drink	free	kitchen	pet fee	pool	spa/sauna	extra info
	C CB	R M	$10 per day	out	X	exercise room, area for walking dogs, close to public park
	C CB	K R M	$5 per day			grassy area for walking dogs, 1 block to public park
R		R M	$5 per stay	in		small dogs only with $20 deposit ($15 is refundable), area for walking dogs
		K R M	$4 per day			3 blocks to public park
		K	$5 per day			dogs allowed in smoking rooms only, area for walking dogs
	C	K R M	$0-$2 per stay			designated dogwalking area, other pets OK w/advance notice, no liability assumed
R	CB	K R M	$7 per day	out	X	area for walking dogs, laundry facilities
	C	K R M	$10 per stay			friendly dogs in residence, easy walking distance to beach–shops–restaurants
	C	K	$10 per stay	out		ocean view, beach access, picnic tables, open area for walking dogs

Maupin — Medford

Deschutes Motel 616 Mill St Maupin, OR 97037	541/395-2626	12 units $40-$65
Oasis Resort, The 609 Hwy 197 South, PO Box 365 Maupin, OR 97037	541/395-2611	12 units $45-$55
Belknap Lodge & Hot Springs PO Box 2001 59296 North Belknap Springs Rd McKenzie Bridge, OR 97413	541/822-3512 541/822-3327 (fax)	2 cabins $35
Country Place, The 56245 Delta Dr McKenzie Bridge, OR 97413	541/822-6008	5 units $68-$220
Baker Street B & B 129 SE Baker St McMinnville, OR 97128	503/472-5575 800/870-5575	5 units $75-95
Paragon Motel 2065 S Hwy 99 W McMinnville, OR 97128	503/472-9493 800/525-5469 503/472-8470 (fax)	55 units $39-$92
Best Western Pony Soldier Inn 2340 Crater Lake Hwy Medford, OR 97504	541/779-2011 800/634-7669	72 units $70-$78
Capri Motel 250 E Barnett Rd Medford, OR 97501	541/773-7796	36 units $30-$55
Cascade Inn Motel 816 N Riverside Ave Medford, OR 97501	541/770-5558	23 units $25-$85

A: Where to Stay in Oregon with Your Dog

food/drink	free	kitchen	pet fee	pool	spa/sauna	extra info
		K R	$10 per stay			area for walking dogs
R	C	K R	$5 per stay			riverside area for walking dogs, RV parking, camp ground, T-shirt shop
		K				dogs allowed in cabins only, laundry facilities, hiking & bike trails for walking dogs
		K		out htd		dogs allowed in 3 cabins, river view, seasonal pool, large area for walking dogs
B & B	FB	K R M			X	dog allowed on balcony of 1 room or enclosed porch of 2 bdrm cottage; dog run avail
R	CB	R M	$6 per day	out		area for walking dogs, adjacent to laundry facilities & restaurant
R & L	CB	R	$10 per day	out	X	small dogs allowed but only in smoking rooms, laundry facilities
	C		$5 per stay	out htd		small area for walking dogs, 3 blocks to public park
		K	$5 per day			dogs allowed for 1 night only, 2 blocks to public park

Medford

Cedar Lodge Motor Inn 518 N Riverside Ave Medford, OR 97501	541/773-7361 800/282-3419 541/776-1033 (fax)	80 units $35-$45
City Center Motel 324 S Central Ave Medford, OR 97501	541/773-6248	18 units $28-$32
Doubletree Inn 200 N Riverside Ave Medford, OR 97501	541/779-5811 800/222-TREE 541/779-7961 (fax)	186 units $61-$84
Fish Lake Resort Hwy 140 (36 miles from Medford) Medford, OR	541/949-8500	10 cabins $40-$90
Howard Prairie Lake Resort Hyatt Prairie Rd, PO Box 4709 Medford, OR 97501	541/773-3619	18 units $75-$85
Knight's Inn Motel 500 N Riverside Ave Medford, OR 97501	541/773-3676 800/626-1900 541/857-0493 (fax)	83 units $37-$45
Mill Wood Inn 1030 N Riverside Ave Medford, OR 97501	541/773-1152 541/773-1152 (fax)	32 units $30-$34
Motel 6 North 2400 Biddle Rd Medford, OR 97504	541/779-0550 800/4-MOTEL-6 541/857-9573 (fax)	116 units $35-43
Motel 6 South 950 Alba Dr Medford, OR 97504	541/773-4290 800/4-MOTEL-6 541/857-9574 (fax)	167 units $32-$45
Oregon Lodge 525 S Riverside Ave Medford, OR 97501	541/772-6133 800/460-OR-LO 541/772-6133 (fax)	38 units $30-$85

A: Where to Stay in Oregon with Your Dog

food/drink	free	kitchen	pet fee	pool	spa/sauna	extra info
R & L	CB	K R M	$10 ref dep	out		pet walking area, BBQ & picnic tables, bike & walking paths, 1-1/2 blocks to park
			$5 per day			2 blocks to public park
2 R & L	C FB	R avail		2 out htd		close to bike path & public park, health club, $79-$84 rates include full breakfast
R		K R	$10 per day			1 or 2 dogs only, on leash at all times, lakeside resort, mini-mart, hiking trails
		K				fully equipped trailers, camp sites, swimming beach, lakeside walking area
	C	R M avail	$100 ref dep	out		riverfront area for walking dogs, laundry facilities
	C	R M	$20 ref dep			laundry facilities, close to riverfront area for walking dogs
	C			out		all queen beds, dog walking area, bike & walking trails nearby
	C			out		1 small dog per room, close to public park, laundry facilities
R	C CB	K	$5 per day			large area for walking dogs, 1/2 mile to public park, laundry facilities

Medford — Merlin

Pear Tree Motel	541/535-4445	46 units
3730 Fern Valley Rd I-5 Exit 24	800/645-7332	$50-$87
Medford, OR 97504	541/535-3960 (fax)	
Reston Hotel	541/779-3141	164 units
2300 Crater Lake Hwy	800/779-7829	$54-$62
Medford, OR 97504	541/779-2623 (fax)	
Rogue Valley Inn	541/772-2800	15 units
2800 E Barnett Rd, PO Box 8228		$55-$68
Medford, OR 97504		
Sierra Inn	541/773-7727	36 units
345 S Central Ave		$25-$48
Medford, OR 97501		
Sis-Q Motel	541/773-8411	12 units
722 S Riverside Ave		$22-$30
Medford, OR 97501		
Tiki Lodge Motel	541/773-4579	28 units
509 N Riverside Ave		$28-$59
Medford, OR 97501	541/773-4579 (fax)	
Waverly Cottage & Suites	541/779-4716	6 units
305 N Grape St		$40-$70
Medford, OR 97501	541/732-1718 (fax)	
Windmill Inn	541/779-0050	123 units
1950 Biddle Rd	800/547-4747	$62-$89
Medford, OR 97504	541/779-0050 (fax)	
Doubletree Ranch	541/476-0120	3 cabins
6000 Abegg Rd		$65-$75
Merlin, OR 97532		
Galice Resort	541/476-3818	6 units
11744 Galice Rd		$45-$139
Merlin, OR 97532	541/471-0188 (fax)	

A: Where to Stay in Oregon with Your Dog

food/drink	free	kitchen	pet fee	pool	spa/sauna	extra info
R	C	R M	$10 per stay	out htd	X	dogs allowed at manager's discretion only, pancake breakfast included, laundry
R & L	C		$10 per stay	in		laundry facilities, area for walking dogs, close to city-wide walking paths
	C	K	$5 per day			private patios, open field for walking dogs, near hospital & public park, weekly rates
	C	K	$3 per day			1 block to public park, laundry facilities
		R M	$5 per day			short drive to public park for walking dogs
R & L	C	R M avail	$5 per stay			no puppies, 2 blocks to public park
	C	K			X	dogs at mgr's discretion only, near public parks, in-room spa, www.aaaabb.com
	C CB	R M.		out htd	X	close to walking & biking paths, bicycles avail, group-senior-AAA discounts
		K	$5 per day			dogs allowed at manager's discretion only, riverfront area & trails for walking dogs
R & L		K				dogs allowed in bunkhouse, cottage & cabins; riverside trails for walking dogs

Merrill — Mt. Vernon

Wild Goose Motel PO Box W Merrill, OR 97633	541/798-5826	11 units $27-$44
Morgan Inn 104 N Columbia Milton-Freewater, OR	541/938-5547 800/533-4017 97862 541/938-7714 (fax)	42 units $45-$105
Out West Motel 84040 Hwy 11 Milton-Freewater, OR 97862	541/938-6647 800/881-6647 541/938-7408 (fax)	10 units $31-$46
Sky Hook Motel 101 Hwy 26, PO Box 84 Mitchell, OR 97750	541/462-3569	6 units $30-$45
Stage Coach Inn Motel 415 Grange Ave Molalla, OR 97038	503/829-4382	32 units $50-$65
College Inn 235 Pacific Ave S Monmouth, OR 97361	503/838-1711 503/838-2370 (fax)	12 units $35-$60
Courtesy Inn 270 N Pacific Ave Monmouth, OR 97361	503/838-4438 503/838-3761 (fax)	35 units $45-$75
Tall Winds Motel 301 Main St (Hwy 97) PO Box 323 Moro, OR 97039	541/565-3519	12 units $30-$60
Mt. Hood Hamlet B & B 6741 Hwy 35 Mt. Hood, OR 97041	541/352-3574 800/407-0570	3 units $95-$125
Blue Mountain Lodge Motel 150 W Main St Mt. Vernon, OR 97865	541/932-4451	13 units $25-$40

food/drink	free	kitchen	pet fee	pool	spa/sauna	extra info
	C	K				riverfront area for walking dogs, trailer spaces also avail
	CB	K	$0-$10/ stay			small dogs only, grassy area for walking dogs, 5 blocks to public park, laundry facilities
	C	R M				area for walking dogs, HBO & Showtime
	C	K	$5 per day			area for walking dogs, public park across highway
	C	K	$5 per day			open field for walking dogs
		K R	$5 per day			5 blocks to public park
R	C	R M	$5 per day			1 dog per room only, close to public park
	C	K R				adjacent to public park for walking dogs
B & B	FB		$5 per day			dog at mgr's discretion only, private baths, dogwalking area, near hiking & fishing
		R				1 block to public park

Mt. Vernon — Newport

Mt. Vernon Motel & Trailer Park 195 N Mountain Blvd Mt. Vernon, OR 97865	541/932-4712	5 units $30-$42
Quick Stop Motel 6453 Dole Rd Myrtle Creek, OR 97457	541/863-4689 541/863-4689 (fax)	12 units $30-$45
Myrtle Trees Motel 1010 8th St Myrtle Point, OR 97458	541/572-5811	29 units $33-$42
Breakers Condominiums, The 48060 Breakers Blvd Neskowin, OR 97149	503/392-3417	11 units $165
Terimore Lodging by the Sea 5105 Crab Ave Netarts, OR 97143	503/842-4623 800/635-1821	26 units $45-$87
Shilo Inn—Newberg 501 Sitka Ave Newberg, OR 97132	503/537-0303 800/222-2244 503/537-0442 (fax)	60 units $65-$99
Towne & Country Motel 1864 Portland Rd (99W) Newberg, OR 97132	503/538-2800	22 units $40-$49
Anchorage Cottages, The 7743 N Coast Hwy Newport, OR 97365	541/265-5463	6 units $64-$86
Green Gables B & B 156 SW Coast St Newport, OR 97365	541/265-9141 800/515-9065	2 units $85-$95

A: Where to Stay in Oregon with Your Dog

food/drink	free	kitchen	pet fee	pool	spa/sauna	extra info
		K				shaded yard for walking dogs, 2 blocks to public park, 1/2 mile north of Mt. Vernon
R	C	K	$3 per day			dogs allowed at manager's discretion only, large yard to walk dog, convenience store
	C	R M	$5 per day			small pets only, 2-1/2 landscaped acres for walking dogs, picnic area
		K				3 bdrm 2 bath townhouses, fully equipped kitchens, located right on the beach
	C	K R	$5 per day			ocean view, beach access, open area for walking dogs, laundry facilities
C CB		R M	$7 per day	out	X	free USA Today newspaper, 24 hr recreation center, laundry facilities
		K				open field for walking dogs, close to public park, cable TV, air conditioning
		K				beach access, fully equipped cottages & townhouses, free firewood, beach & pet towels
B & B	FB	R M			X	1-1/2 blocks to beach, ocean view, in-room spa, cable TV & VCR, bookstore on-site

Newport

Hallmark Resort 744 SW Elizabeth St Newport, OR 97365	541/265-2600 888/448-4449 541/265-9449 (fax)	158 units $89-$199
Holiday Inn 3019 N Coast Hwy 101 Newport, OR 97365	541/265-9411 800/ HOLIDAY 541/265-8773 (fax)	148 units $74-$124
Money Saver Motel 861 SW Coast Hwy Newport, OR 97365	541/265-2277	42 units $30-$85
Newport City Center Motel 538 SW Coast Hwy Newport, OR 97365	541/265-7381 800/628-9665 541/265-7749 (fax)	30 units $50-$86
Newport Motor Inn 1311 N Coast Hwy Newport, OR 97365	541/265-8516	39 units $32-$62
Penny Saver Motel 710 N Coast Hwy Newport, OR 97365	541/265-6631 800/477-3669	46 units $38-$96
Shilo Inn–Newport Oceanfront Resort 536 SW Elizabeth Newport, OR 97365	541/265-7701 800/222-2244 541/265-5687 (fax)	179 units $109-$149
Summer Wind Motel 728 N Coast Hwy Newport, OR 97365	541/265-8076	33 units $30-$70
Surf 'n' Sand Motel 8143 N. Coast Hwy 101 Newport, OR 97365	541/265-2215	18 units $63-$96

food/drink	free	kitchen	pet fee	pool	spa/sauna	extra info
	C CB	K R M	$5 per day	in	X	pet area for walking dogs, oceanfront rooms, fitness room, easy beach access
R & L	C	R M		out htd	X	dogs allowed in smoking rooms only, near grassy area & beach for walking dogs
	C	K	$5 per day			refundable pet deposit & damage contract, laundry facilities
	CB	K	$5 per day			dogs under 20 lbs only, open area for walking dogs, 1-1/2 blocks from beach
R & L	C		$4 per day			open field for walking dogs, facilities to clean fish & cook crabs, laundry facilities
	CB	K R M	$5 per stay			dogs under 20 lbs only, yard for walking dogs, 7 blocks from beach
R & L	C	R M	$7 per day	2 in		free USA Today newspaper, ocean view, in-room VCR
	C	K	$5 per stay			quiet area for walking dogs, 7 blocks to beach
		K	$3 per day			1-3/4 acres for walking dogs, ocean view, beach access

Newport — O'Brien

Traveler's Inn 606 SW Coast Hwy Newport, OR 97365	541/265-7723 800/615-2627	42 units $35-$65
Vikings Cottages, The 729 NW Coast Hwy Newport, OR 97365	541/265-2477 800/480-2477	14 units $65-$95
Willers Motel 754 SW Coast Hwy Newport, OR 97365	541/265-2241 800/945-5377 541/265-8235 (fax)	37 units $38-$109
City Center Motel 750 Connecticut St North Bend, OR 97459	541/756-5118	18 units $29-$38
Itty Bitty Inn B & B Motel 1504 Sherman, Hwy 101 North Bend, OR 97459	541/756-6398 888/276-9253	5 units $39-$45
Parkside Motel 1480 Sherman Ave North Bend, OR 97459	541/756-4124 541/756-1771 (fax)	16 units $32-$85
Pony Village Motor Lodge Virginia Ave North Bend, OR 97459	541/756-3191 541/756-5818 (fax)	119 units $43-$75
Powder River Motel I-84 Exit 285, PO Box 269 North Powder, OR 97867	541/898-2829 or 541/898-2740	12 units $25-$38
Arrow Head Motel 710 Emmison Ave Nyssa, OR 97913	541/372-3942	7 units $40
Madrone Motel 32429 Redwood Hwy O'Brien, OR 97534	541/596-2498	4 units $22-$40

food/drink	free	kitchen	pet fee	pool	spa/sauna	extra info
	C	R M	$5 per day			ocean view, beach access
		K				oceanfront cottages, no dogs alone in room, area for walking dogs
	C	K	$4 per day			laundry facilities, yard for walking dogs, 1-1/2 blocks to beach
	CB	R M	$25 ref dep			2 blocks to public park, clean & quiet
		R	$5 per day			small dogs only, room fee includes breakfast at nearby restaurant, near public parks
	C	K R M	$5 per stay			rooms & fully equipped apts, laundry facilities, area for walking dogs
R & L		R M avail	$3 per day			area for walking dogs, next to large mall, 5-10 minute drive to dunes & beach
		R avail				laundry facilities, 1-1/2 blocks to riverfront for walking dogs
	C	R M				area for walking dogs, close to public park
	C	K	$5 per day			rooms & cabin, area for walking dogs

Oakland — Ontario

Ranch Motel 581 John Long Rd Oakland, OR 97462	541/849-2126 541/849-2379 (fax)	25 units $31-$65
Arbor Inn 48229 Hwy 58 Oakridge, OR 97463	541/782-2611 800/505-9047 541/782-3618 (fax)	15 units $28-$38
Best Western Oakridge Inn 47433 Hwy 58 Oakridge, OR 97463	541/782-2212 800/528-1234 541/782-2811 (fax)	40 units $54-$76
Oakridge Motel 48197 Hwy 58 East, PO Box 773 Oakridge, OR 97463	541/782-2432	10 units $29-$57
Ridgeview Motel 47465 Hwy 58 Oakridge, OR 97463	541/782-3430	10 units $28-$35
Best Western Inn 251 Goodfellow Ln Ontario, OR 97914	541/889-2600 800/828-0364 541/889-2259 (fax)	61 units $51-$95
Budget Inn 1737 N Oregon St Ontario, OR 97914	541/889-3101 800/905-0024 541/889-4150 (fax)	26 units $38-$65
Carlile Motel 589 N Oregon St Ontario, OR 97914	541/889-8658 800/640-8658	19 units $35-$60
Colonial Inn of Ontario 1395 Tapadera Ave Ontario, OR 97914	541/889-9615 800/727-5014 541/889-9615 (fax)	89 units $29-$70
Holiday Inn Ontario 1249 Tapadera Ave Ontario, OR 97914	541/889-8621 800/525-5333 541/889-8023 (fax)	98 units $52-$75

A: Where to Stay in Oregon with Your Dog

food/drink	free	kitchen	pet fee	pool	spa/sauna	extra info
	C	R M avail	out htd			I-5 exit 148 in Rice Hill, area for walking dogs, laundry facilities
	C	K	$50 ref dep			area near creek for walking dogs
	CB	K R	$5 per day	out	X	small dogs only, area for walking dogs
R	C	R				dogs allowed at manager's discretion only, large area for walking dogs
	C					area for walking dogs, 2 blocks to riverside park & walking trails
	C CB	R M	$75 ref dep	in	X	open area for walking dogs, near river, laundry facilities, exercise room
	C	K R	ref dep	out		laundry facilities, open lot for walking dogs, close to state park
	C	K R M	$5 per day			small dogs only, AAA rates, large open area for walking dogs
	C CB			in	X	area for walking dogs, close to river
R & L	C		$5 per day	out htd	X	large open lot for walking dogs

Ontario — Otter Rock

Holiday Motel 615 E Idaho Ave Ontario, OR 97914	541/889-9188 541/889-4303 (fax)	72 units $35-$56
Motel 6–Ontario 275 NE 12th St Ontario, OR 97914	541/889-6617 800/4-MOTEL-6 541/889-8232 (fax)	125 units $29-$99
North Star Motel 1751 N Oregon St Ontario, OR 97914	541/889-5314	12 units $25-$36
Oregon Trail Motel 92 E Idaho Ave Ontario, OR 97914	541/889-8633 800/895-7945 541/889-7096 (fax)	30 units $28-$65
Plaza Motel 1144 SW 4th Ave Ontario, OR 97914	541/889-9641	25 units $25
Stockman's Motel 81 SW 1st St Ontario, OR 97914	541/889-4446 541/889-4114 (fax)	28 units $$32-$45
Super 8 Motel 266 Goodfellow Ln Ontario, OR 97914	541/889-8282 800/800-8000 541/881-1400 (fax)	63 units $43-$55
Val-U Inn Motel 1900 Clackamette Dr Oregon City, OR 97045	503/655-7141 800/443-7777 503/655-1927 (fax)	117 units $61-$69
Alpine Chalets 7045 Otter Crest Lp, Box 23 Otter Rock, OR 97369	541/765-2572 800/825-5768 541/765-3135 (fax)	11 units $75-$90

food/drink	free	kitchen	pet fee	pool	spa/sauna	extra info
R	C			out htd		area for walking dogs, short drive to public park
	C			out		laundry facilities, open field for walking dogs
	C	K				laundry facilities, area for walking dogs, close to public park
	C	K				area for walking dogs, close to public park
	C	K R M	$10 ref dep			weekly & monthly rates, area for walking dogs, close to hospital & public park
	C	R	ref dep			refundable pet deposit, area for walking dogs, close to public park
	C CB	R M	ref dep	in	X	laundry facilities, exercise room, small area for walking dogs
R & L	C	R M avail	$5 per day	out	X	river view, area along river for walking dogs
		K	$10 per day			private park on premises w/picnic area, beach access www.netbridge.net/alpine

Oxbow — Pendleton

Hells Canyon Motel & RV Park PO Box 243 Oxbow, OR 97840	541/785-3393 800/453-3393	6 units $45-$60
Anchorage Motel 6585 Pacific Ave, PO Box 626 Pacific City, OR 97135	503/965-6773 800/941-6250	10 units $35-$69
Inn at Pacific City 35215 Brooten Rd PO Box 1000 Pacific City, OR 97135	503/965-6366 888/PAC-CITY 503/965-6812 (fax)	16 units $49-$89
7 Inn I-84 Barnhart Rd Exit 202 PO Box 1065 Pendleton, OR 97801	541/276-4711	50 units $91-$97
Budget Inn 1807 SE Court Ave Pendleton, OR 97801	541/276-4521	30 units $31-$51
Chaparral Motel 620 SW Tutuilla Pendleton, OR 97801	541/276-8654 541/276-5808 (fax)	51 units $36-$56
Doubletree Hotel Pendleton 304 SE Nye Ave Pendleton, OR 97801	541/276-6111 800/222-TREE 541/278-2413 (fax)	168 units $59-$81
Let 'Er Buck Motel 205 SE Dorion Ave Pendleton, OR 97801	541/276-3293	35 units $25-$40
Longhorn Motel 411 SW Dorion Ave Pendleton, OR 97801	541/276-7531 541/278-7889 (fax)	36 units $28-$51

A: Where to Stay in Oregon with Your Dog

food/drink	free	kitchen	pet fee	pool	spa/sauna	extra info
		K				fully equipped cottages, creekside area for walking dogs
	C	K	$3 per day			area to walk dogs, quiet location, 4 blocks to beach, full kitchens, family suites
	C	K R M	$6 per day			5 blocks from beach, open area for walking dogs, close to shops & restaurants
	C	K	$2 per day			laundry facilities, area for walking dogs
	C	R	$5 per day			laundry facilities
R	C	K R avail	$5 per day			senior discount, creekside area for walking dogs
R & L	C		$20 ref dep	out	X	laundry facilities, area for walking dogs
	C	K R	$5 per day			laundry facilities, 4 blocks to public park
	C	R	ref dep			1 block to riverfront trail for walking dogs

Pendleton — Port Orford

Motel 6–Pendleton 325 SE Nye Ave Pendleton, OR 97801	541/276-3160 800/4-MOTEL-6 541/276-7526 (fax)	122 units $36-$49
Pendleton Tapadera Motel 105 SE Court Ave Pendleton, OR 97801	541/276-3231 800/722-8277 541/276-0754 (fax)	47 units $37-$61
Pillars Motel 1816 SE Court Ave Pendleton, OR 97801	541/276-6241	14 units $21-$36
Vagabond Inn 201 SW Court Ave Pendleton, OR 97801	541/276-5252 800/522-1555 541/278-1213 (fax)	51 units $31-$57
Galaxie Motel 104 S 20th St Philomath, OR 97370	541/929-4334 541/929-4334 (fax)	15 units $30-$65
Phoenix Motel 510 N Main St Phoenix, OR 97535	541/535-1555 541/512-0706 (fax)	21 units $42
Pilot Rock Motel 326 NE 4th St, PO Box Q Pilot Rock, OR 97868	541/443-2851	8 units $30-$53
Castaway by the Sea Motel 545 W. 5th St, PO Box 844 Port Orford, OR 97465	541/332-4502 541/332-9303 (fax)	13 units $45-$80
Humbug Mountain Lodge 39292 Hwy 101 Port Orford, OR 97465	541/332-1021	9 units $30-$65
Sea Crest Motel 44 Hwy 101 South, PO Box C Port Orford, OR 97465	541/332-3040 888/332-3040	18 units $55-$85

A: Where to Stay in Oregon with Your Dog

food/drink	free	kitchen	pet fee	pool	spa/sauna	extra info
	C			out		laundry facilities, open field for walking dogs
R & L	C	R	$5 per stay			1/2 block to public park for walking dogs, free passes at nearby health club & pool
	C	R M	$2 per day			dogs allowed at manager's discretion only, weekly rates, area for walking dogs
	CB	R	$5 per day	out		laundry facilities, riverfront area for walking dogs
		K R M				area for walking dogs, close to public park
		K	$5-$8/ day	out	X	small dogs only, area for walking dogs
		K R M	$0-5 per stay			area for walking dogs, also handmade "Shaker-style" dog sweaters for sale
	C	K	$5 per day			ocean view, easy beach access
		K				rooms & cabins, lakeside area for walking dogs, fishing, hiking trails nearby
	C	R avail				1 small dog only, woods & open field for walking dogs, seacrest@harborside.com

Port Orford — Portland

Shoreline Motel 206 6th St Port Orford, OR 97465	541/332-2903	13 units $36-$46
4th Avenue Motel 1889 SW 4th Ave Portland, OR 97201	503/226-7646 503/226-7647 (fax)	21 units $35-$70
5th Avenue Suites Hotel 506 SW Washington Portland, OR 97204	503/222-0001 800/711-2971 503/222-0004 (fax)	221 units $175-$385
6th Avenue Motel 2221 SW 6th Ave Portland, OR 97201	503/226-2979	29 units $45-$55
99 Motel 405 NE Columbia Blvd Portland, OR 97211	503/289-9999 503/286-8834 (fax)	60 units $35-$59
Aladdin Motor Inn 8905 SW 30th Ave Portland, OR 97219	503/246-8241 800/292-4466 503/244-1939 (fax)	52 units $40-$70
Benson Hotel 309 SW Broadway Portland, OR 97205	503/228-2000 800/426-0670 503/226-4603 (fax)	297 units $190-$700
Best Western Heritage Inn 4319 NW Yeon Ave Portland, OR 97210	503/497-9044 800/528-1234 503/497-1030 (fax)	65 units $62-$125
Best Western Inn at the Convention Center 420 NE Holladay St Portland, OR 97232	503/233-6331 800/528-1234 503/233-2677 (fax)	97 units $65-$85

A: Where to Stay in Oregon with Your Dog

food/drink	free	kitchen	pet fee	pool	spa/sauna	extra info
		K	$7 per stay			ocean view, across street from beach
		K R M				small dogs only, close to Waterfront Park for walking dogs, laundry facilities
R & L	C CB	R M avail				small dogs only, evening wine-tasting, 5 blocks to Waterfront Park
R & L	C		$5 per day			small dogs only
	C CB	R M	$5-$10/ day			2 miles to waterfront area for walking dogs
	C	K	$5 per day			small dogs only, laundry facilities, in-room spas, area for walking dogs
R & L	CB		$50 per stay			exercise room, 7 blocks to Waterfront Park for walking dogs
	CB	K		in	X	yard for walking dogs, laundry facilities
R			$6 per day			dogs at manager's discretion only, laundry facilities, 4 blocks to public park

Portland

Best Western Inn at the Meadows 1215 N Hayden Meadows Dr Portland, OR 97217	503/286-9600 800/528-1234 503/286-8020 (fax)	146 units $79-$150
Budget Value Viking Motel 6701 N Interstate Ave Portland, OR 97217	503/285-6687 800/308-5097 503/285-1680 (fax)	25 units $38-$48
Comfort Inn—Convention Center 431 NE Multnomah St Portland, OR 97232	503/233-7933 800/228-5150 503/233-6921 (fax)	79 units $79-$125
Cypress Inns 809 SW King Ave Portland, OR 97205	503/226-6288 800/532-9543 503/274-0038 (fax)	83 units $49-$119
Delta Inn 9930 N Whitaker Rd Portland, OR 97217	503/289-1800 800/833-1800 503/289-3778 (fax)	213 units $60-$75
Doubletree Hotel– Jantzen Beach 909 N Hayden Island Dr Portland, OR 97217	503/283-4466 800/222-TREE 503/283-4743 (fax)	320 units $85-$175
Doubletree Hotel– Portland Lloyd Center 1000 NE Multnomah Blvd Portland, OR 97202	503/281-6111 800-222-TREE 503/249-3137 (fax)	476 units $155-$575
Doubletree Hotel- Columbia River 1401 N Hayden Island Dr Portland, OR 97217	503/283-2111 800/222-TREE 503/283-4718 (fax)	351 units $85-$160

A: Where to Stay in Oregon with Your Dog

food/drink	free	kitchen	pet fee	pool	spa/sauna	extra info
	CB	R M	$22 per stay		X	laundry facilities, small area for walking dogs, 2 blocks to public park
	C	K R	fee varies	out htd		seasonal swimming pool, laundry facilities, 10 minute walk to public park
	C CB	R M		out		dogs allowed in smoking rooms only, in-room spa, 2 blocks to public park
	C CB	K	$10 per day			laundry facilities, 4 blocks from Washington Park for walking dogs
	C CB	K	$10 per day			laundry facilities, wheelchair access rooms, adjacent to public park, airport shuttle
R & L		R		out	X	in-room spa, exercise room, river view, area for walking dogs
3 R & 2 L	C	R		out		laundry facilities, in-room spa, exercise room, public park across street
2 R & L	C	K R M	$15 per stay	out	X	river view, 3 miles of walking paths along the river, guest laundry service

Portland

Holiday Inn Express	503/492-4000	71 units
2323 NE 181st St	800-HOLIDAY	$70-$125
Portland, OR 97230	503/492-3271 (fax)	
Hotel Vintage Plaza	503/228-1212	107 units
422 SW Broadway	800/243-0555	$165-$300
Portland, OR 97205	503/228-3598 (fax)	
Howard Johnson	503/255-6722	137 units
Airport Hotel	800/345-3896	$80-$125
7101 NE 82nd Ave	503/254-3370 (fax)	
Portland, OR 97220		
Imperial Hotel	503/228-7221	136 units
400 SW Broadway	800/452-2323	$80-$105
Portland, OR 97205	503/223-4551 (fax)	
Knickerbocker Motor Motel	503/285-6637	23 units
4739 N Interstate Ave		$40-$65
Portland, OR 97217		
Lamplighter Motel	503/297-2211	56 units
10207 SW Park Way		$40
Portland, OR 97225		
Mallory Hotel	503/223-6311	136 units
729 SW 15th Ave	800/228-8657	$75-$120
Portland, OR 97205	503/223-0522 (fax)	
Mark Spencer Hotel	503/224-3293	101 units
409 SW 11th Ave	800/548-3934	$75-$120
Portland, OR 97205	503/223-7848 (fax)	
Marriott–Portland Hotel	503/226-7600	509 units
1401 SW Front Ave	800/228-9290	$165-$400
Portland, OR 97201	503/499-6357 (fax)	

A: Where to Stay in Oregon with Your Dog

food/drink	free	kitchen	pet fee	pool	spa/sauna	extra info
	C CB	K		in	X	fresh-baked cookies 6-9 P.M., area for walking dogs, public park nearby
R & L	CB	R			X	complimentary wine-tasting, close to Waterfront Park, 1 small dog only
R & L	C		$10 per day	out	X	area for walking dogs, laundry facilities, in-room movies, off track betting
R & L		R	$10 per stay			laundry service, 7 blocks to Waterfront Park
		K				area for walking dogs, close to public park, shops & restaurants
	C	K	$5-$10/ day			small area for walking dogs
R & L		R	$10 per stay			2 blocks to open area for walking dogs, 15 blocks to Waterfront Park
	C CB	K	$200 ref dep			laundry facilities, $10 pass to health club & pool, 2 blocks to public park
R & L	C	R avail		in	X	river view, exercise room, laundry facilities, adjacent to Waterfront Park

Portland

Motel 6	503/238-0600	69 units
3104 SE Powell Blvd		$49-$62
Portland, OR 97202	503/238-7167 (fax)	
Oxford Suites	503/283-3030	135 units
12226 N Jantzen Dr	800/548-7848	$75-$115
Portland, OR 97217	503/735-1661 (fax)	
Portland Rose Motel	503/244-0107	37 units
8920 SW Barbur Blvd		$35-$65
Portland, OR 97219		
Portland Travelodge Suites	503/788-9394	39 units
7740 SE Powell Blvd	800/578-7878	$70-$75
Portland, OR 97206	503/788-9378 (fax)	
Quality Inn–Portland Airport	503/256-4111	120 units
8247 NE Sandy Blvd	800/246-4649	$65-$100
Portland, OR 97220	503/254-1507 (fax)	
Ranch Inn Motel	503/246-3375	20 units
10138 SW Barbur Blvd		$33-$40
Portland, OR 97219		
Red Lion Inn–Coliseum	503/235-8311	212 units
1225 N Thunderbird Way	800-222-TREE	$69-$110
Portland, OR 97227	503/232-2670 (fax)	
Residence Inn by Marriott–	503/288-1400	168 units
Lloyd Center	800/331-3131	$109-$175
1710 NE Multnomah Blvd	503/288-0241 (fax)	
Portland, OR 97232		
Riverside Inn, The	503/221-0711	140 units
50 SW Morrison St	800/648-6440	$89-$160
Portland, OR 97204	503/274-0312 (fax)	

A: Where to Stay in Oregon with Your Dog

food/drink	free	kitchen	pet fee	pool	spa/sauna	extra info
	C			out		AARP discount avail, across the street from public park & track
	C	R M	$15 per stay	in	X	dogs under 25 lbs only, full breakfast included, also hors d'oeuvres with wine or beer
		K				area for walking dogs, laundry facilities
	C CB	R M	$25 ref dep		X	small area for walking dogs, laundry facilities, 2 blocks to public park
R & L	C CB	R M	$10 per stay	out		laundry facilities, airport shuttle, in-room spa, area for walking dogs
		K R				dogs allowed for 1 to 2 nights only, area for walking dogs
R & L	C	R avail	$10 per stay	out		river & city views, easy I-5 access, dogwalking area, close to Waterfront Park
	C CB	K	$10 per day	out	X	1 to 2 dogs only, small area for walking dogs, 4 blocks to park, laundry facilities
R & L	C	K	$100 ref dep			dogs under 50 lbs only, near health club & pool, riverfront walking path

Portland — Prairie City

Rodeway Inn–Convention Center 1506 NE 2nd Ave Portland, OR 97232	503/231-7665 800/228-2000 503/236-6040 (fax)	44 units $50-$65
Shilo Inn Portland/Beaverton 9900 SW Canyon Rd Portland, OR 97225	503/297-2551 800/222-2244 503/297-7708 (fax)	142 units $89-$125
Silver Cloud Inn–Downtown 2426 NW Vaughn St Portland, OR 97210	503/242-2400 800/205-6939 503/242-1770 (fax)	81 units $85-$109
Sullivan's Gulch B & B 1744 NE Clackamas St Portland, OR 97232	503/331-1104 503/331-1575 (fax)	3 units $65-$75
Super 8 Motel 11011 NE Holman St Portland, OR 97220	503/257-8988 800/800-8000 503/253-1427 (fax)	80 units $57-$85
Travelodge Portland Airport 9727 NE Sandy Blvd Portland, OR 97220	503/255-1400 800/578-7878 503/256-3842 (fax)	163 units $49-$84
Tudor House B & B 2321 NE 28th Ave Portland, OR 97212	503/287-9476 800/786-9476 503/288-8363 (fax)	4 units $70-$100
Vagabond Inn 518 NE Holladay St Portland, OR 97232	503/234-4391 800/522-1555 503/236-8870 (fax)	35 units $59-$69
Riverside School House Bed & Breakfast County Rd #61, Rt 2 Box 700 Prairie City, OR 97869	541/820-4731	1 house $65-$100

A: Where to Stay in Oregon with Your Dog

food/drink	free	kitchen	pet fee	pool	spa/sauna	extra info
	C CB	R	$7 per day		X	area for walking dogs, laundry facilities, close to large pet store
R & L	C CB	R M	$7 per day	out	X	free USA Today newspaper, breakfast buffet, exercise room
	C CB	K R M	$10 per day		X	fitness center, free parking, laundry facilities, close to public park
	CB	R				quiet streets for dogwalking, friendly resident dog, www.teleport.com/~thegulch/
	C CB		ref dep			small area for walking dogs, close to bike path, "park & fly" airport shuttle service
R & L	C CB	R	$11 per day	out htd		in-room jacuzzi, area for walking dogs, laundry facilities
B & B	FB	K	$5 per day			dogs allowed at manager's discretion only, large back yard, 4 blocks to public park
	CB	R	$10 per day			close to public park
B & B	FB					100 yr. old schoolhouse on ranch near river, sleeps 4, lots of area for walking dogs

Prairie City — Redmond

Strawberry Mountain Inn Bed & Breakfast HCR 77 #940 Hwy 26 E Prairie City, OR 97869	541/820-4522 800/545-6913	5 units $65-$125
Carolina Motel 1050 E 3rd St Prineville, OR 97754	541/447-4152 541/447-6876 (fax)	26 units $38-$59
City Center Motel 509 E 3rd St Prineville, OR 97754	541/447-5522 541/447-7739 (fax)	20 units $32-$49
Ochoco Inn & Motel 123 E 3rd St Prineville, OR 97754	541/447-6231	47 units $39-$56
Rustler's Roost Motel 960 W 3rd St Prineville, OR 97754	541/447-4185	20 units $40-$60
Prospect Historical Hotel & Motel 391 Mill Creek Dr PO Box 50 Prospect, OR 97536	541/560-3664 800/944-6490 541/560-3825 (fax)	22 units $60-$80
Union Creek Resort 56484 Hwy 62 Prospect, OR 97536	541/560-3565 or 541/560-3339	23 units $38-$85
Rainier Budget Inn 120 A St West, PO Box 370 Rainier, OR 97048	503/556-4231 503/556-2608 (fax)	26 units $35-$85
City Center Motel 350 NW 6th St Redmond, OR 97756	541/548-3447	14 units $35-$59

food/drink	free	kitchen	pet fee	pool	spa/sauna	extra info
B & B	FB					linda.strawberrymt.inn@worldnet.att.net, dogs allowed in separate heated facility
	C CB	K	$5 per day			laundry facilities, creekside area for walking dogs, close to public park & waterfall
	C	R M				adjacent to public parks & swimming pool, email: ccmotel@bendnet.com
R & L	C	K	$5 per day			area for walking dogs, close to walking trails & parks
	C	K R M	$5 per day			close to riverfront & open field for walking dogs
R	C	K				area for walking dogs
R		K	$5 per day			dogs allowed in fully equipped cabins, creek & riverside trails to walk dogs
		K R M	$5 per day			river view, close to public park
		K	$5 per day			large area for walking dogs, close to public park

Redmond — Reedsport

Hub Motel, The 1128 N Hwy 97 Redmond, OR 97756	541/548-2101 800/7-THE HUB 541/923-4167 (fax)	30 units $38-$64
Redmond Inn 1545 Hwy 97 S Redmond, OR 97756	541/548-1091 800/833-3259 541/548-0415 (fax)	46 units $44-$68
Anchor Bay Inn 1821 Hwy 101 Reedsport, OR 97467	541/271-2149 800/767-1821 541/271-1802 (fax)	21 units $39-$63
Best Budget Inn 1894 Winchester Ave Reedsport, OR 97467	541/271-3686 541/271-4019 (fax)	23 units $28-$85
Best Western Salbasgeon Inn 1400 Hwy 101 S Reedsport, OR 97467	541/271-4831 800/528-1234 541/271-4831 (fax)	56 units $68-$125
Fir Grove Motel 2178 Winchester Ave Reedsport, OR 97467	541/271-4848 541/271-2330 (fax)	19 units $36-$85
Pacific Sands Hometel 76347 Hwy 101 Reedsport, OR 97467	541/271-4894	35 units $28-$38
Salbasgeon Inn of the Umpqua 45209 Hwy 38 Reedsport, OR 97467	541/271-2025	12 units $60-$98
Salty Seagull Motel 1806 Winchester Ave Reedsport, OR 97467	541/271-3729 800/476-8336	9 units $35-$458

A: Where to Stay in Oregon with Your Dog

food/drink	free	kitchen	pet fee	pool	spa/sauna	extra info
R	C	K R M	$5 per day			area for walking dogs
R & L	C CB	R M	$5 per day	out		large area for walking dogs, in-room jacuzzi in one room, children under 12 free
	CB	K	$5 per day	out		laundry facilities, area for walking dogs, www.presys.com/chwy/r/reedspor.htm
	CB	K R M	$3 per day			area for walking dogs, 1 block to public park
	C CB		$5 per day	in	X	fitness center, grassy area near the river for walking dogs, laundry facilities
	CB	K		out htd		small dog allowed at mgr's discretion only, seasonal pool, small area to walk dogs
R		R				$1.99 breakfast specials in restaurant, area for walking dogs, 1/2 mile from beach
	C	K	$5 per day			large riverside area for walking dogs, river & mountain views
	C	K				all 3-room suites, complete kitchens, fenced area for walking dogs, laundry

Reedsport — Rockaway Beach

Tropicana Motel 1593 Hwy 101 Reedsport, OR 97467	541/271-3671 800/799-9970 541/271-3671 (fax)	41 units $32-$50
Hitching Post Motel 1st & Main, PO Box 166 Richland, OR 97870	541/893-6176	18 units $37-$65
Wagontire Motel & Cafe HC 74 Box 500 Riley, OR 97758	541/493-2317 800/550-2317	6 units $25-$45
101 Motel 530 N Hwy 101 Rockaway Beach, OR 97136	503/355-2420 888/878-3973	7 units $35-$55
Getaway Motel on the Beach 621 S Pacific St Rockaway Beach, OR 97136	503/355-2501 800/756-5552	13 units $60-$110
Idle-Nook Motel 141 NW 20th, PO Box 236 Rockaway Beach, OR 97136	503/355-2007	4 units $40-$54
Ocean Locomotion Motel 19130 Alder Ave Rockaway Beach, OR 97136	503/355-2093	8 units $48-$95
Ocean Spray Motel 505 N Pacific St Rockaway Beach, OR 97136	503/355-2237	8 units $45-$75
Rock Creek Inn 145 N Miller, PO Box 728 Rockaway Beach, OR 97136	503/355-8488 800/710-7625	22 units $85-$130
Sand Dollar Motel 105 NW 23rd Ave Rockaway Beach, OR 97136	503/355-2301 503/355-8462 (fax)	10 units $35-$90

food/drink	free	kitchen	pet fee	pool	spa/sauna	extra info
	CB	K	$3 per day	out		area for walking dogs, 5 minute walk to public park
	C	K R	$0-$5/ day			rooms & cabins, area for walking dogs, close to public park, 1 mile from river
R						RV park, service station, landing strip, designated pet "relief" & exercise area
		K	$5.25 per day			fully equipped kitchens, area for walking dogs, 1-1/2 blocks to beach
		K	$10-$15/ day			fully equipped beachfront condominiums, quiet neighborhood
		K	$4 per day			one adult dog only (no puppies), fully equipped beachfront cottages
	C	K	$5 1st day			www.inninnsandouts.com/ property/ocean_locomotion _motel.html
		K	$5-$10/ day			2 small or 1 large dog only, beachfront location
	C	K R M				dogs under 15 lbs allowed at mgr's discretion only, fully equipped condominiums
	C	K	$5-$15/ stay			ocean view, easy beach access

Rockaway Beach — Roseburg

Sea Treasures Inn	503/355-8220	14 units
301 N Miller St, PO Box 755	800/444-1864	$48-$78
Rockaway Beach, OR 97136	503/355-8042 (fax)	
Silver Sands Motel	503/355-2206	64 units
215 S. Pacific Ave, PO Box 61	800/457-8972	$82-$114
Rockaway Beach, OR 97136	503/355-9690 (fax)	
Surfside Oceanfront	503/355-2312	80 units
Resort Motel	800/243-7786	$48-$150
101 NW 11th Ave		
Rockaway Beach, OR 97136		
Twin Rocks Motel	503/355-2391	5 units
7925 Minnehaha St		$74-$84
Rockaway Beach, OR 97136		
Best Western Douglas Inn	541/673-6625	52 units
511 SE Stephens St	800/528-1234	$45-$72
Roseburg, OR 97470	541/673-6625 (fax)	
Best Western Garden	541/672-1601	121 units
Villa Motel	800/547-3446	$62-$102
760 NW Garden Valley Blvd	541/672-1316 (fax)	
Roseburg, OR 97470		
Budget 16 Motel	541/673-5556	48 units
1067 NE Stephens St	800/414-1648	$30-$57
Roseburg, OR 97470	541/673-7942 (fax)	
Casa Loma Motel	541/673-5569	18 units
1107 NE Stephens St		$32-$45
Roseburg, OR 97470		
Dunes Motel	541/672-6684	46 units
610 W Madrone St	800/260-9973	$40-$60
Roseburg, OR 97470	541/672-6684 (fax)	

A: Where to Stay in Oregon with Your Dog

food/drink	free	kitchen	pet fee	pool	spa/sauna	extra info
	C	K R M	$5 1-3 days			1/2 block to beach, near restaurants
	C	K R	$5 per stay	in	X	1 dog under 25 lbs only, ocean view, beach access
	C	K	$10 per stay	in		beachfront location, ocean & lake views
		K	$5 1st day			$2 ea additional day, fully equipped beachfront cabins, area to walk dog, ocean view
	C				X	close to public park
CB		R M avail	$5 per day	out	X	fitness room, nearby area for walking dogs with trail to park, laundry facilities
	C	K R M		out htd		pool open May 24-Oct 1, area for walking dogs, 4 blocks to public park
	C	K	$5 per day		X	area for walking dogs
	C CB	R M				fresh-baked cookies in lobby each afternoon, 1 block to public park, covered parking

Roseburg — Salem

Howard Johnson–Roseburg 978 NE Stephens St Roseburg, OR 97470	541/673-5082 541/673-6594 (fax)	31 units $60-$110
Motel Orleans 427 NW Garden Valley Blvd Roseburg, OR 97470	541/673-5561 800/626-1900 541/957-0318 (fax)	72 units $35-$63
New Vista Motel 1183 NE Stephens St Roseburg, OR 97470	541/673-2736	15 units $25-$69
Rose City Motel 1142 NE Stephens St Roseburg, OR 97470	541/673-8209	11 units $35-$75
Shady Oaks Motel 2954 Old Hwy 99 S Roseburg, OR 97470	541/672-2608	12 units $37-$55
Shamrock Motel 2484 Old Hwy 99 South Roseburg, OR 97470	541/672-9183	14 units $35-$45
Windmill Inn of Roseburg 1450 NW Mulholland Dr Roseburg, OR 97470	541/673-0901 800/547-4747 541/673-0901 (fax)	128 units $65-$79
Arrowhead Motel 204 W 2nd St, PO Box 714 Rufus, OR 97050	541/739-2354	12 units $31-$51
Tyee Motel 304-1/2 East 1st, PO Box 175 Rufus, OR 97050	541/739-2310 541/739-2288 (fax)	18 units $35-$55
City Center Motel 510 Liberty St SE Salem, OR 97301	503/364-0121 800/289-0121 503/581-0554 (fax)	30 units $42-$55

A: Where to Stay in Oregon with Your Dog

food/drink	free	kitchen	pet fee	pool	spa/sauna	extra info
	C CB	K R M	$5 per day			free pass to athletic club & pool, small area for walking dogs, 2-1/2 blocks to park
	C	R M	ref dep			laundry facilities, AAA & senior rates
		R M avail	$5- $10/ day			area for walking dogs
		K				large field for walking dogs
	C					AAA rates, area for walking dogs, large landscaped yard with BBQ & picnic tables
		K	$5 per day			area for walking dogs
	C CB	R M avail		out	X	fitness room, laundry facilities, bicycles avail, group-senior-AAA discounts
		K	$5 per day			small dogs only, rooms & cabins, lots of open area for walking dogs
	C	K R M	$10 per stay			laundry facilities, arcade & pool table, area for walking dogs
	CB		$3 per day			laundry facilities, small area for walking dogs, close to public park

Salem

Holiday Lodge 1400 Hawthorne Ave NE Salem, OR 97301	503/585-2323 800/543-5071 503/585-2153 (fax)	54 units $40-$50
Mar-Don Motel 3355 Portland Rd NE Salem, OR 97303	503/585-2089	14 units $35-$53
Motel 6 1401 Hawthorne Ave NE Salem, OR 97301	503/371-8024 800/4-MOTEL-6 503/371-7691 (fax)	115 units $32-$44
Motel 6–Salem South 2250 Mission St SE Salem, OR 97302	503/588-7191 800/4-MOTEL-6 503/588-0486 (fax)	78 units $34-$47
Oregon Capital Inn 745 Commercial St SE Salem, OR 97301	503/363-2451 503/363-3536 (fax)	109 units $35-$40
Phoenix Inn–Salem 4370 Commercial St SE Salem, OR 97302	503/588-9220 800/445-4498 503/585-3616 (fax)	89 units $61-$105
Ramada Inn 200 Commercial St SE Salem, OR 97301	503/363-4123 800/2-RAMADA 503/363-8993 (fax)	114 units $45-$175
Salem Grand Hotel 1555 State St Salem, OR 97301	503/581-2466 503/581-2811 (fax)	42 units $38-$65
State House B & B 2146 State St Salem, OR 97301	503/588-1340 800/800-6712 503/585-8812 (fax)	4 units $50-$70
Super 8 Motel 1288 Hawthorne Ave NE Salem, OR 97301	503/370-8888 800/800-8000 503/370-8927 (fax)	79 units $45-$71

food/drink	free	kitchen	pet fee	pool	spa/sauna	extra info
R & L	C		ref dep	out		dogs allowed at manager's discretion only
		K	$3 per day			dogs allowed at manager's discretion only, weekly rates avail, area for walking dogs
	C			out		small dogs only, area for walking dogs
	C			out		AARP discount avail, area for walking dogs, 5 blocks to public park
			$10 per stay			laundry facilities, area for walking dogs, close to Riverfront Park & Bush Park
	CB	R M	$10 per day	in	X	laundry facilities, exercise room, area for walking dogs
R & L	C CB	K R M	$10 per stay	out	X	dogs allowed at manager's discretion only, seasonal pool, adjacent to public park
	C	R avail	$5 per day	out		
B & B	FB	K R M				small dogs allowed at mgr's discretion only, creekside dog walking area & paths
	C CB	R	ref dep	in	X	laundry facilities, area for walking dogs

Salem — Seaside

Tiki Lodge Motel	503/581-4441	50 units
3705 Market St NE	800/438-8458	$36-$65
Salem, OR 97301	503/581-4442 (fax)	
Best Western Sandy Inn	503/668-7100	45 units
37465 Hwy 26	800/528-1234	$65-$68
Sandy, OR 97055	503/668-0624 (fax)	
Brookside B & B	503/668-4766	5 units
45232 SE Paha Loop		$35-$65
Sandy, OR 97055		
Malarkey Ranch B & B	503/543-5244	4 units
55948 Columbia River Hwy		$55-$60
Scappoose, OR 97056	503/543-5224 (fax)	
Best Western Ocean	503/738-3334	104 units
View Resort	800/234-8439	$69-$265
414 N Prom	503/738-3264 (fax)	
Seaside, OR 97138		
Budget Inn of Seaside	503/738-5221	23 units
521 Beach Dr	800/479-5191	$58-$143
Seaside, OR 97138		
Bungalow City Motel	503/738-5191	18 units
1000 N Holladay Dr	800/479-5191	$45-$57
Seaside, OR 97138		
City Center Motel	503/738-6377	40 units
250 1st Ave	800/479-5191	$67-$153
Seaside, OR 97138		
Coast River Too	503/738-8474	5 units
800 S Holladay Dr	800/479-5191	$63-171
Seaside, OR 97138		

food/drink	free	kitchen	pet fee	pool	spa/sauna	extra info
	C	K		out	X	small dogs only, area for walking dogs
	CB	R M		in	X	small dogs only, exercise room, laundry facilities, nature area for walking dogs
B & B	FB					dogs allowed at manager's discretion only, children OK, rural area for walking dogs
B & B	FB			out		large area for walking dogs, horseback riding & trails
R & L	C	K	$15 per day	in	X	dogs allowed Sep–May only, next to promenade that runs along beach for 2 miles
	C	K	$3-5 per day			1/2 block to beach, laundry facilities, close to shops–restaurants–arcades
	C	K	$5 per day			area for walking dogs, 4 blocks to beach
	C	K	$5 per day	in	X	laundry facilities, 1-1/2 blocks to beach, adjacent to shops–restaurants–arcades
	C	K	$5 per day			area for walking dogs, 5 blocks to beach, 4 blocks to downtown

Seaside

Comfort Inn Boardwalk 545 Broadway Seaside, OR 97138	503/738-3011 800/228-5150 503/738-4397 (fax)	65 units $89-$150
Driftwood Motel 825 N Holladay Dr Seaside, OR 97138	503/717-0331 800/479-5191	13 units $48-$70
Edgewater Inn on the Prom 341 S Prom Seaside, OR 97138	503/738-4142 800/822-3170 503/738-4171 (fax)	14 units $99-$159
Guest House B & B, The 486 Necanicum Dr Seaside, OR 97138	503/717-0495 800/340-8150	4 units $65-$95
Lanai Oceanfront Condominiums 3140 Sunset Blvd Seaside, OR 97138	503/738-6343 800/738-2683 503/738-6344 (fax)	17 units $45-$85
Oceanside Vacation Rentals 110 5th Ave Seaside, OR 97138	503/738-7764 800/840-7764	10 units $60-$200
Pine Cove Motel 2481 Hwy 101 N Seaside, OR 97138	503/738-5243	12 units $27-$54
Rogers Inn & Vacation Home Rentals 446 S Downing St Seaside, OR 97138	503/738-7367 888-717-7367 503/717-1618 (fax)	21 units $85-$525
Seaside Convention Center Inn 441 2nd Ave Seaside, OR 97138	503/738-9581 800/699-5070 503/738-3212 (fax)	48 units $69-$149

A: Where to Stay in Oregon with Your Dog

food/drink	free	kitchen	pet fee	pool	spa/sauna	extra info
	CB	K R M		in	X	river view, laundry facilities, 3 blocks to beach, next to promenade along beach
	C	K R	$5 per day			area for walking dogs, approximately 7 blocks to beach
	C	K	$10 per day			ocean view, in-room jacuzzi, fireplace, on the promenade that runs 2 miles along beach
B & B	FB					dogs allowed in fenced yard & heated garage, 2 blocks to beach, evening snacks
		K	$10 per stay	out		small dogs only, no dogs left alone in rooms, fully equipped condo units
		K				ocean view, jacuzzi, laundry facilities, from beachfront to within 3 blocks of beach
	C	K R M	$5 per day			laundry facilities, area for walking dogs
		K	$30 per stay			motel units, fully equipped kitchens & laundry facilities, vacation houses also avail
	C CB	K	$5 per day	in	X	laundry facilities, 2 blocks to beach & promenade, close to shops & restaurants

223

Seaside — Sisters

Seasider II Motel 210 N Downing St Seaside, OR 97138	503/738-7622 800/305-3718	12 units $45-$75
Seasider Motel 110 5th Ave Seaside, OR 97138	503/738-7764 800/840-7764	10 units $30-$80
Seaview Inn 120 9th Ave Seaside, OR 97138	503/738-5371 800/479-5191	23 units $63-$161
Royal Coachman Motel 21906 Hwy 62, PO Box 509 Shady Cove, OR 97539	541/878-2481	15 units $41-$54
Two Pines Motel 21331 Hwy 62, PO Box 906 Shady Cove, OR 97539	541/878-2511 541/878-5023 (fax)	10 units $44-$125
Nordic Motel 310 N Water St Silverton, OR 97381	503/873-5058	8 units $39-$49
Best Western Ponderosa Lodge 505 Hwy 20 W, PO Box 218 Sisters, OR 97759	541/549-1234 888/549-4321 541/549-0409 (fax)	48 units $84-$99
Black Butte Accommodations PO Box 366 Sisters, OR 97759	541/549-3433	1 house $160-$183
Sisters Comfort Inn 540 Hwy 20 W, PO Box 938 Sisters, OR 97759	541/549-7829 541/549-1807 (fax)	50 units $69-$79

A: Where to Stay in Oregon with Your Dog

food/drink	free	kitchen	pet fee	pool	spa/sauna	extra info
	C	R M	$6 per stay			area for walking dogs, 2 blocks to beach
	CB	R M	$5 per day			dogs allowed at manager's discretion only, ocean view, laundry facilities
	C	K	$5 per day			ocean view, 1 block to boardwalk & beach
	C	K R M				small dogs only, area for walking dogs, next to river & 2 restaurants
R	C	K R				full kitchens in some rooms, dogs at manager's discretion only, dog walking area
	C	K				dog walking area, access to riverfront path across street
	C CB		$5 per day	out	X	open area for walking dogs, near Metolius River, close to golf-skiing-horseback riding
		K		in htd		fully equipped 3 bdrm 2 bath house on golf course, lots of walking paths, laundry
	C CB	K		in	X	dogs allowed at manager's discretion only, large areas for walking dogs

Sisters — Springfield

Sisters Motor Lodge	541/549-2551	11 units
511 W Cascade, PO Box 28		$50-$75
Sisters, OR 97759		
Squaw Creek B & B	541/549-4312	3 units
68733 Junipine Lane	800/930-0055	$80-$85
PO Box 1993	541/549-4312 (fax)	
Sisters, OR 97759		
Solace by the Sea B & B	541/867-3566	3 units
9602 S Coast Hwy	888-476-5223	$135-$175
South Beach, OR 97366	541/867-3599 (fax)	
Thiel Shores Motel	541/867-4305	6 units
9812 S Coast Hwy		$45-$90
South Beach, OR 97366		
Asher Motel	541/468-2053	4 units
106 Willow St, PO Box 115		$30-$40
Spray, OR 97874		
Doubletree Hotel	541/726-8181	234 units
Eugene/Springfield	800/222-TREE	$74-$125
3280 Gateway Rd	541/747-1866 (fax)	
Springfield, OR 97477		
Motel 6–Eugene/Springfield	541/741-1105	131 units
3752 International Ct	800/4-MOTEL-6	$33-$45
Springfield, OR 97477	541/741-6007 (fax)	
Motel Orleans	541/746-1314	71 units
3315 Gateway St	800/626-1900	$42-$69
Springfield, OR 97477	541/746-3884 (fax)	
Rodeway Inn	541/746-8471	58 units
3480 Hutton St	800/363-8471	$60-$100
Springfield, OR 97477	541/747-1541 (fax)	

food/drink	free	kitchen	pet fee	pool	spa/sauna	extra info
	C CB	K	$5 per day			dogs allowed at manager's discretion only, mountain view, areas for walking dogs
B & B	FB				X	dogs allowed at manager's discretion only, area for walking dogs
B & B	FB		$10 per day			open-air kennel with dog house provided for guests' dogs, beach access
	C	K R M	$5 per day			dogs allowed at manager's discretion only, easy beach access, laundry facilities
						area for walking dogs, close to restaurant
2 R & L	C	R M avail		out	X	large area for walking dogs, airport shuttle, 5 blocks to bike & walking paths
	C			out		area for walking dogs
	C	R M	ref dep	out		laundry facilities, AAA & senior rates
	C CB	R M avail	$10 per day	in		laundry facilities, large open field for walking dogs

Springfield — Sutherlin

Shilo Inn–Eugene/ Springfield 3350 Gateway Springfield, OR 97477	541/747-0332 800/222-2244 541/726-0587 (fax)	143 units $59-$119
Village Inn Motel 1875 Mohawk Blvd Springfield, OR 97477	541/747-4546 800/327-6871 541/747-4452 (fax)	70 units $47-$75
Village Inn Motel 535 S Hwy 30 St. Helens, OR 97051	503/397-1490 503/397-6840 (fax)	52 units $34-$61
Bird & Hat Inn B & B 717 N 3rd Ave Stayton, OR 97383	503/769-7817	3 units $55-$65
Silver Mountain B & B 4672 Drift Creek Rd SE Sublimity, OR 97385	503/769-7127 800/952-3905 503/769-3549 (fax)	2 units $60-$75
Lodge at Summer Lake 36980 Hwy 31 Summer Lake, OR 97640	541/943-3993 541/943-3993 (fax)	12 units $39-$175
Summer Lake B & B 31501 Hwy 31 Summer Lake, OR 97640	541/943-3983 800/261-2778	6 units $50-$85
Twin Lakes Resort 11200 S Century Dr, PO Box 3550 Sunriver, OR 97707	541-593-6526 541/410-4688 (fax)	14 units $75-$115
Microtel Inn–Sutherlin 1400 Hospitality Place Sutherlin, OR 97479	541/459-2236 888/771-7171 541/459-1751 (fax)	80 units $50-$60

A: Where to Stay in Oregon with Your Dog

food/drink	free	kitchen	pet fee	pool	spa/sauna	extra info
R & L	C CB	K	$7 per day	out		laundry facilities, free USA Today newspaper, children under 12 free
R & L	C	K		out	X	laundry facilities, area for walking dogs
R & L		K	$3 per day			area for walking dogs
B & B	FB					landscaped yard, fish ponds, resident cat, 2 blocks to public park
B & B	FB	K		out htd	X	400-acre farm with lots of room for walking dogs
R		K	$5 per stay			2 units include breakfast or dinner, also 3 bdrm house, thelodge31@aol.com
R			$10 per stay		X	rooms & cabins, breakfast & dinner avail for additional fee, swimming dock on lake
		K	$5 per day			lakefront cabins & RV park, surrounded by national forest
	C					I-5 Exit 136, open Feb 1998, large area for walking dogs, short drive to parks & river

Sutherlin — The Dalles

Town & Country Motel 1386 W Central Ave Sutherlin, OR 97479	541/459-9615 800/459-9615	18 units $39-$59
Sweet Home Inn 805 Long St Sweet Home, OR 97386	541/367-5137 800/595-8859 541/367-8859 (fax)	31 units $49-$69
Willow Motel 3026 Hwy 20 Sweet Home, OR 97386	541/367-2205 541/367-8994 (fax)	11 units $30-$40
Barretts of Harris Street 100 Harris St The Dalles, OR 97058	541/296-2027 800/298-4885 (code 12)	1 apt $65-$85
Best Eastern Oregon Motor Motel, 200 W 2nd St The Dalles, OR 97058	541/296-9111 541/296-9111 (fax)	54 units $39-$49
Best Western Umatilla House 112 W 2nd St The Dalles, OR 97058	541/296-9107 800/722-8277 541/296-3002 (fax)	65 units $52-$79
Captain Gray's Guest House 210 W 4th St The Dalles, OR 97058	541/298-8222 800/448-4729 541/298-8222 (fax)	3 units $50-$80
Days Inn 2500 W 6th St The Dalles, OR 97058	541/296-1191 800/448-5544 360/891-0182 (fax)	70 units $51-$59
Inn at The Dalles 3550 SE Frontage Rd The Dalles, OR 97058	541/296-1167 800/982-3496 541/296-3920 (fax)	44 units $28-$70
Quality Inn 2114 W 6th St The Dalles, OR 97058	541/298-5161 800/848-9378 541/298-6411 (fax)	85 units $59-$69

A: Where to Stay in Oregon with Your Dog

food/drink	free	kitchen	pet fee	pool	spa/sauna	extra info
	C		$5 per day			1 small dog only, area for walking dogs, 1/2 block to public park
	C	K	$5 per stay		X	laundry facilities, area for walking dogs, close to public park
		K				small dogs only, area for walking dogs
		K			X	dog at mgr's discretion only, 2 bdrm fully equipped apt, 7 night min, near park & trails
	C	R M	$5 per day	out htd		weekly rates avail, area for walking dogs, 1/2 mile to river
R & L	C	K R avail		out		area for walking dogs, close to public park
B & B	FB	K			X	laundry facilities, fenced back yard, close to public park, captgray@gorge.net
	CB		$10 per day	out	X	seasonal pool, microwave avail in breakfast area for guest use
	C	K R M		in htd		river view, area for walking dogs, 1/2 mile to riverside park
R & L	C	R	$2 per day	out	X	laundry facilities, 2 blocks to open field for walking dogs

The Dalles — Tillamook

Shamrock Motel	541/296-5464	25 units
118 W 4th St		$32-$53
The Dalles, OR 97058	541/ (fax)	
Shilo Inn–The Dalles	541/298-5502	112 units
3223 Bret Clodfelter Way	800/222-2244	$55-$115
The Dalles, OR 97058	541/298-4673 (fax)	
Best Western Chateau 290	503/620-2030	68 units
17993 SW Lower Boones	800/528-1234	$62-$89
Ferry Rd	503/620-2030 (fax)	
Tigard, OR 97224		
Embassy Suites Hotel–	503/644-4000	354 units
Portland/Washington Square	800/EMBASSY	$132-$147
9000 SW Washington Sq Rd	503/641-4654 (fax)	
Tigard, OR 97223		
Motel 6–Tigard West	503/684-0760	80 units
17959 SW McEwan Rd	800/4-MOTEL-6	$43-$59
Tigard, OR 97224	503/968-2539 (fax)	
Quality Inn Portland South	503/620-3460	118 units
7300 SW Hazel Fern Rd	800/291-8860	$62-$129
Tigard, OR 97223	503/639-9130 (fax)	
Shilo Inn–Tigard/	503/620-4320	77 units
Washington Square	800/222-2244	$65-$105
10830 SW Greenburg Rd	503-620-8277 (fax)	
Tigard, OR 97223		
Sea Lion Motel	503/842-5477	7 units
4951 Netarts Hwy W.		$49-$69
Tillamook, OR 97141	503/842-8867 (fax)	
Shilo Inn–Tillamook	503/842-7971	100 units
2515 N Main St	800/222-2244	$65-$109
Tillamook, OR 97141	503/842-7960 (fax)	

A: Where to Stay in Oregon with Your Dog

food/drink	free	kitchen	pet fee	pool	spa/sauna	extra info
	C	K R M	$5 per day			close to public park for walking dogs
R & L	C CB	R M	$7 per day	out	X	free USA Today newspaper, exercise room, laundry facilities
	CB	R M	$6 per day	out	X	small dogs allowed, dogs in smoking rooms only, laundry facilities
R & L	FB	R M		in	X	all suites, designated dog walking area, close to public park & trails
	C			out htd		laundry facilities, grassy area for walking dogs
	C CB	R M	$10 per day avail	out	X	exercise room, laundry facilities, large area for walking dogs
	C CB	R M	$7 per day		X	24 hr recreation center, free USA Today newspaper, laundry facilities
	C	K				located 6 miles west of Tillamook in Netarts, full kitchens, 1 block to beach
R & L	C	R M	$7 per day	in	X	24 hr recreation center, free USA Today newspaper, laundry facilities

Tillamook — Troutdale

Three Capes Inn at Netarts 4800 Netarts Hwy W Tillamook, OR 97141	503/842-4003	8 units $50-$65
Tillamook Inn 1810 Hwy 101 N Tillamook, OR 97141	503/842-4413 503/842-3179 (fax)	27 units $46-$90
Western Royal Inn 1125 N Main St Tillamook, OR 97141	503/842-8844 800/624-2912 503/842-8876 (fax)	40 units $55-$105
Cannon Village Motel 3163 S Hemlock St, PO Box 162 Tolovana Park, OR 97145	503/436-2317	11 units $60-$130
Tolovana Inn 3400 S. Hemlock St Tolovana Park, OR 97145	503/436-2211 800/333-8890 503/436-0134 (fax)	178 units $68-$249
Obstinate J Ranch 29680 Hwy 62 Trail, OR 97541	541/878-2718 541/878-4389 (fax)	4 units $80-$110
Rogue River Osprey House 24954 Hwy 62 Trail, OR 97541	541/878-3555 541/878-3555 (fax)	1 house $80-$120
Burns West Motel 790 NW Frontage Rd Troutdale, OR 97060	503/667-6212 503/665-3746 (fax)	60 units $43-$54
Motel 6–Portland/Troutdale 1610 NW Frontage Rd Troutdale, OR 97060	503/665-2254 800/4-MOTEL-6 503/666-1849 (fax)	123 units $-38-$50
Phoenix Inn–Troutdale 477 NW Phoenix Dr Troutdale, OR 97060	503/669-6500 800/824-6824 503/669-3500 (fax)	73 units $66-$115

234

A: Where to Stay in Oregon with Your Dog

food/drink	free	kitchen	pet fee	pool	spa/sauna	extra info
	C	K	$5 per day			mini-apartments, large yard & hiking trails for walking dogs, 1-1/2 blocks to beach
	C	K	$10 per stay			large yard & riverfront trails for walking dogs, $5 daypass avail for YMCA pool
	C	R M	$5 per stay		X	dogs allowed at manager's discretion only, area for walking dogs
	C	K R M	$5 per stay			coffeepot & hotplates also avail, designated pet area, located 1 block from beach
R & L	C	K	$10 per day	in	X	oceanfront, laundry facilities, licensed massage therapist
		K		out	X	fully equipped houses, tennis court, 1 mile of river frontage, ojranch@aol.com
R & L	C	K R M	ref dep			river frontage, dogs allowed at mgr's discretion only, fully equipped 2 bdrm house
R & L			$6 per day			laundry facilities, grassy area for walking dogs, close to outlet stores
	C			out		1 small dog only, laundry facilities, area for walking dogs, open field next door
	CB	R M	$10 per day	in	X	exercise room, laundry facilities, area for walking dogs, close to public park

Tualatin — Waldport

Sweetbrier Inn 7125 SW Nyberg Rd Tualatin, OR 97062	503/692-5800 800/551-9167 503/691-2894 (fax)	132 units $68-$110
Antlers Inn Main & Alba, PO Box 97 Ukiah, OR 97880	541/427-3492	12 units $25-$55
High Heather Inn 705 Willamette Ave Umatilla, OR 97882	541/922-4871 800/447-7529 541/922-4773 (fax)	68 units $40-$80
Rest-a-Bit Motel 1370 6th St Umatilla, OR 97882	541/922-3271 800/423-9913 541/922-3271 (fax)	36 units $38-$110
Tillicum Motor Inn 1481 6th St Umatilla, OR 97882	541/922-3236 541/922-5889 (fax)	79 units $35-$62
Unity Motel & RV Park 302 Main, PO Box 87 Unity, OR 97884	541/446-3431	7 units $25-$80
Vernonia Inn 900 Madison Ave Vernonia, OR 97064	503/429-4006 800/354-9494	15 units $45-$80
Riverside Inn 45441 McKenzie Hwy Vida, OR 97488	541/896-3218	4 units $40
Wayfarer Resort 46725 Goodpasture Rd Vida, OR 97488	541/896-3613 800/627-3613	13 units $70-$195
Alsea Manor Motel 190 SW Arrow (Hwy 101), PO Box 466 Waldport, OR 97394	541/563-3249	16 units $55-$65

food/drink	free	kitchen	pet fee	pool	spa/sauna	extra info
R & L	C	K	$100 ref dep	out	htd	exercise room, woods & grass area for walking dogs, close to public park
	C		$5 per day			dogs allowed at manager's discretion only, close to public park for walking dogs
R & L	C	K	$10 per stay	out	X	golf course, off-track betting, area for walking dogs, 1-1/2 blocks to Columbia river
	C	K R M				river view from some units, close to public park for walking dogs
	C	K	$10 per day	out		area for walking dogs, laundry facilities
		K R				area for walking dogs, short drive to national forest & wilderness area
	CB					in-room hot tubs, within 4 blocks of 2 public parks, 1 block to shops & restaurants
R & L						across street from river, area for walking dogs, next to Willamette Nat'l Forest
		K	$10 per day			hot tub in 1 unit, creek & river for swimming, lots of room to walk dogs
	C		$5 per day			area for walking dogs, 1 block to bay shore

Waldport — Welches

Bayshore Inn 902 NW Bayshore Dr Waldport, OR 97394	541/563-3202 800/526-9586 541/563-5641 (fax)	92 units $80-$180
Edgewater Cottages 3978 SW Pacific Coast Hwy Waldport, OR 97394	541/563-2240	8 units $60-$130
Sundown Motel 5050 SW Hwy 101 Waldport, OR 97394	541/563-3018 800/535-0192	8 units $53-$85
Waldport Motel 170 SW Arrow (Hwy 101) PO Box 514 Waldport, OR 97394	541/563-3035	13 units $45-$55
Cherokee Mingo Motel & Hot Tub, The 102 N Alder & Hwy 82 PO Box 146 Wallowa, OR 97885	541/886-2021	12 units $35-$55
Kah-Nee-Ta Resort 100 Main St, PO Box K Warm Springs, OR 97761	541/553-1112 800/831-0100 541/553-1071 (fax)	20 units $55-$90
Ray's Tavern & Motel 45 NE Skipanon Dr Warrenton, OR 97146	503/861-2566	9 units $38-$48
Shilo Inn–Warrenton 1609 E Harbor Dr Warrenton, OR 97146	503/861-2181 800/222-2244 503/861-2980 (fax)	62 units $89-$145
Old Welches Inn 26401 E Welches Rd Welches, OR 97067	503/622-3754 503/622-5370 (fax)	5 units $130-$175

238

A: Where to Stay in Oregon with Your Dog

food/drink	free	kitchen	pet fee	pool	spa/sauna	extra info
R & L	C	R avail	$10 per stay	out		bay view, easy access to bay shore area for walking dogs, 5 minute walk to ocean
		K	$5-$10/ day			ocean view, fireplaces, beach access for walking dogs
	C	K R M	$6 per day			ocean view, located right on the beach for walking dogs
		K	$3 per day			small dogs only, area for walking dogs, easy access to shoreline of bay
	CB	R M	$3 per stay		X	area for walking dogs, close to cafe & laundromat
				out	X	dogs allowed in teepees & RV park only, area for walking dogs
	C	R				area for walking dogs, close to beach for walking dogs
R & L	C	R M	$7 per day	in	X	24 hr recreation center, free USA Today newspaper, laundry facilities
	C	K M				dogs allowed in riverfront cottage only, fully equipped kitchen, fenced yard

239

Westlake — Wilsonville

Siltcoos Lake Resort & Motel 82855 Fir St, PO Box 36 Westlake, OR 97493	541/997-3741	8 units $30-$65
Westlake Resort 4785 Laurel Ave, PO Box 25 Westlake, OR 97493	541/997-3722	9 units $40-$60
Westport Motel Hwy 30, PO Box 5036 Westport, OR 97016	503/455-2212	8 units $45-$80
View of the West— A Country Inn 294 Hall St, PO Box 178 Wheeler, OR 97147	503/368-5766 503/368-4806 (fax)	12 units $65-$120
Best Western Willamette Inn 30800 SW Parkway Ave Wilsonville, OR 97070	503/682-2288 888/682-0101 503/682-1088 (fax)	63 units $70-$98
Burns Bros Motel 8750 SW Elligsen Rd Wilsonville, OR 97070	503/682-2123 800/909-2876 503/682-1212 (fax)	75 units' $35-$52
Holiday Inn 25425 SW 95th Ave Wilsonville, OR 97070	503/682-2211 800/465-4329 503/682-5596 (fax)	169 units $59-$125
Motel Orleans 8815 SW Sun Pl Wilsonville, OR 97070	503/682-3184 800/626-1900 503/682-2351 (fax)	79 units $38-$70
Snooz-Inn 30245 SW Parkway Ave Wilsonville, OR 97070	503/682-2333 800/343-1553 503/682-0980 (fax)	57 units $36-$45

A: Where to Stay in Oregon with Your Dog

food/drink	free	kitchen	pet fee	pool	spa/sauna	extra info
	C	K				area for walking dogs, pet-sitting services & kennels available for additional fee
		K				weekly rates, lakefront cabins with fully equipped kitchens, dog walking area
		K R M	$3 per day			BBQ & picnic table, dog walking area, close to public playground
	CB	K	$100 ref dep			small dogs only, bay & mtn views, area for walking dogs, near park & waterfront
	CB			out	X	dogs under 25 lbs only, seasonal pool, fitness room, large area for walking dogs
R	C		$3 per day	out htd		laundry facilities, grassy area for walking dogs
R & L	C	R M	$10 per day	in	X	$50 refundable deposit, laundry facilities, area for walking dogs, close to park
	C	R M	ref dep	out	X	refundable pet deposit, AAA & senior rates, laundry facilities
	C	R M	$3 per day	out		small dogs only, near public park, 10% discount coupons for restaurant next door

Wilsonville — Woodburn

Super 8 Motel 25438 SW Parkway Ave Wilsonville, OR 97070	503/682-2088 800/800-8000 503/682-0453 (fax)	72 units $40-$56
Discovery Point Resort 242 Discovery Pt Ln HC 81 Box 242 Winchester Bay, OR 97467	541/271-3443 541/271-9357 (fax)	7 cabins $68-$88
Salmon Harbor Motel 265 8th St, PO Box 1486 Winchester Bay, OR 97467	541/271-2732	9 units $25-$40
Winchester Bay Rodeway Inn 390 Broadway, PO Box 1037 Winchester Bay, OR 97467	541/271-4871 800/228-2000 541/271-4871 (fax)	50 units $54-$95
Safari Inn 101 NE Main St Winston, OR 97496	541/679-6736	18 units $34-$45
Sweet Breeze Inn II 251 NE Main St PO Box 2260 Winston, OR 97496	541/679-2420 888/672-2420 541/679-2415 (fax)	32 units $53-$74
Our Shepherd's Inn 159 Bloom Rd Wolf Creek, OR 97497	541/866-2501 800/388-3756	12 units $30-$45
Comfort Inn Woodburn 120 NE Arney Rd Woodburn, OR 97071	503/982-1727 800/228-5150 503/982-0355 (fax)	49 units $66-$110
Fairway Inn Motel 2450 Country Club Ct Woodburn, OR 97071	503/981-3211 800/981-2466 503/981-1935 (fax)	46 units $36-$55

A: Where to Stay in Oregon with Your Dog

food/drink	free	kitchen	pet fee	pool	spa/sauna	extra info
	C		ref dep			refundable deposit, area for walking dogs, Super 8 VIP discounts, laundry facilities
		K	ref dep			fully equipped bayfront cabins & RV park, across street from beach & jetty
C FB		K	$5 per stay			area for walking dogs, 1-1/2 blocks from harbor
C CB		K	$3 per day			in-room spas, area for walking dogs, 1 block to harbor, 1 mile to beach
C						area for walking dogs, 3 blks to public park, mail address: 1733 Winston Section Rd
C		R M	$5 per stay			area for walking dogs
C CB		K R			X	area for walking dogs, developing a creekside park on the property
C CB		K R M		out htd	X	fresh-baked cookies every evening, spa suites, laundry facilities, dogwalking area
C		R M avail		out		dog at mgr's discretion only, laundry facilities, open field for walking dogs

Yachats — Yamhill

Adobe Resort, The	541/547-3141	93 units
1555 Hwy 101, PO Box 219	800/522-3623	$59-$150
Yachats, OR 97498	541/547-4234 (fax)	
Beachcombers Motel	541/547-3432	5 units
95500 Hwy 101 S		$30-$75
Yachats, OR 97498		
Fireside Resort Motel, The	541/547-3636	46 units
1881 N Hwy 101, PO Box 313	800/336-3573	$60-$135
Yachats, OR 97498	541/547-3152 (fax)	
Holiday Inn Market & Motel	541/547-3120	7 units
5933 Hwy 101		$55-$60
Yachats, OR 97498		
See Vue Motel	541/547-3227	11 units
95590 Hwy 101 S		$42-$65
Yachats, OR 97498		
Shamrock Lodgettes	541/547-3312	19 units
105 Hwy 101 S, PO Box 346	800/845-5028	$71-$112
Yachats, OR 97498	541/547-3843 (fax)	
Silver Surf Motel	541/547-3175	24 units
3767 Hwy 101 N	800/281-5723	$85-$89
Yachats, OR 97498		
Yachats Inn	541/547-3456	20 units
331 S Hwy 101, PO Box 307		$61-$88
Yachats, OR 97498	541/547-4331 (fax)	
Flying M Ranch	503/662-3222	31 units
23029 NW Flying M Rd		$60-$200
Yamhill, OR 97148	503/662-3202 (fax)	

A: Where to Stay in Oregon with Your Dog

food/drink	free	kitchen	pet fee	pool	spa/sauna	extra info
R & L	C	K R	$8 per day		X	dogs allowed in 12 units only, sauna & spa, beach access & walking trail
		K R	$6 per day			1 to 2 dogs only, ocean view, area for walking dogs, easy beach access, next to store
	C	K R	$7 per day			rooms & cabins (2 nite min), ocean view, in-room spa, walking trail, beach access
	C	K	$5 per day			cabins with full kitchens, fireplaces, ocean view, easy beach access
		K R	$5 per day			ocean view, theme rooms, large yard for walking dogs, beach access
	C	K	$3 per day		X	dogs in cabins only, area for walking dogs, ocean view, easy beach & river access
	C	K	$5 1-2 days	in	X	ocean view, laundry facilities, beachfront access for walking dogs
	C	K	$5 per day	in htd	X	ocean view, rec room with common kitchen, beachfront area for walking dogs
R & L		K				rooms & cabins, private airstrip, swimming pond, horseback trail rides

B: Emergency Clinics

Time is a critical factor when your pet needs emergency medical care. Your best bet for quickly finding a veterinary clinic is the local phone book. Always call ahead, even during normal office hours. That gives their staff a chance to prepare so that any lifesaving procedures that the doctor may deem necessary will be ready the minute your pet arrives. They can also give directions so that you don't waste time or get lost along the way.

Even though the nearest clinic may not be open at the moment, many do offer 24 hour emergency service. When you call after normal business hours, their answering service takes down your name, the nature of the emergency, and the phone number you're calling from. That information is immediately relayed to the doctor who is "on call" at the time. He or she then calls you back with either instructions for handling the situation yourself or directions for meeting the doctor at the clinic.

Three clinics, in Portland and Corvallis, are open 24 hours/day, every day of the year. Several more "after-hours" clinics are open all night during the week, and 24 hour/day on weekends and holidays. These are located in Aloha (west of Portland), Salem, Springfield, and Tualatin (south of Portland). High Desert Veterinary in Bend, while not actually open around the clock for walk-in business, provides immediate 24 hour emergency care. And in Klamath Falls, a group of clinics share emergency duties.

Oregon's 24 hour and after hours clinics:

Aloha (12 miles west of Portland)
Dove Lewis Emergency Animal Hospital–Aloha
503/645-5800   18990 SW Shaw
          6 P.M.—Midnight on Monday-Saturday
          Noon—8 P.M. on Sunday & holidays

Bend
High Desert Veterinary
541/382-9262   60885 SE 27th St
          8 A.M.—6 P.M. Monday—Friday
          9 A.M.—5 P.M. Saturday
          24 hour emergency service
After regular clinic hours, call ahead—you'll get the answering service. Leave a phone number where the doctor can call you right back.

Corvallis
Animal Emergency & Critical Care Center
(also Willamette Veterinary Clinic)
541/753-5750   650 SW Third St
          24 hours/day, 7 days/week, 365 days/year
          Veterinarian on premises at all times

Klamath Falls
Animal Emergency Services
541/882-9005   Service hours: 5 P.M.—8 A.M.
on weeknights; Saturday Noon—Monday 8 A.M.
Leave your phone number; the doctor on duty will
call you back within 15 minutes.

Portland—Northwest
Dove Lewis Emergency Animal Hospital-Downtown
503/228-7281   1984 NW Pettygrove St
   24 hours/day, 7 days/week, 365 days/year
   Veterinarian on premises at all times

Portland—Southeast
Southeast Portland Animal Hospital
503/255-8139   13830 SE Stark St
   24 hours/day, 7 days/week, 365 days/year
   Veterinarian on premises at all times

Salem
Salem Veterinary Emergency Clinic
503/588-8082   450 Pine St SE
   5 P.M.—8 A.M. on weeknights
   24 hours on weekends & holidays

Springfield
Emergency Veterinary Hospital
541/746-0112   103 "Q" St
   6 P.M.—8 A.M. Monday—Friday
   Saturday noon—Monday 8 A.M.
   24 hours on holidays

Tualatin (10 miles south of Portland)
Emergency Veterinary Clinic of Tualatin
503/691-7922   19314 SW Mohave Ct
   6 P.M.—8 A.M. on weeknights
   24 hours on weekends & holidays

249

C: Some Useful Books

During the writing of this book, I discovered a number of other useful volumes about dogs. Their topics range from dog training to first aid procedures to why your best pal thinks like a dog instead of a human. To learn more, check these books out—you'll find a wealth of information just waiting for you at the library or bookstore.

Here are some personal favorites:

ASPCA Complete Dog Care Manual by Bruce Fogle, D.V.M. This oversized book is full of photographs that beautifully illustrate dog behavior, body language, training methods, and first aid techniques.

Dogs & Kids, Parenting Tips by Bardi McLennan. Lots of helpful information for integrating a dog—and especially a puppy—into your family. Includes some great insights into solving or preventing common behavior problems.

Dogs and the Law by Anmarie Barrie, Esq. This slim volume will give you a real education on your rights and responsibilities as a dog owner.

Dr. Jim's Animal Clinic for Dogs by Jim Humphries, D.V.M. Written in the form of questions and answers from the author's talk radio show. Humorous style makes this book easy to read as well as informative.

Dr. Pitcairn's Complete Guide to Natural Health for Dogs & Cats by Richard H. Pitcairn, D.V.M., Ph.D. and Susan Hubble Pitcairn. This is one volume that is used *a lot* in our household. Full of information about how important a nutritious diet is for your pet's lifelong health, it even includes recipes for preparing nutritionally balanced dog food, whether you are dealing with pet allergies or just want to explore alternatives to commercial dog chow. Also includes an extensive reference section on common health problems as well as medical emergencies.

I Just Got a Puppy. What Do I Do? by Mordecai Siegal and Matthew Margolis. Zeroes right in on what the new owner of a puppy needs to do, know, provide, and train to bring up your new "baby."

The Canine Good Citizen by Jack and Wendy Volhard. The authors' training methods are based on understanding how your dog views the world: what factors motivate him to either good or bad

252

behavior, and how you can steer him toward the behavior you want.

The Dog Care Book by Sheldon L. Gerstenfeld, V.M.D. This medical reference book includes a wonderfully clear set of diagnostic charts that help you determine whether your dog's emergency situation is minor, serious, or life-threatening—and what to do about it.

The Home Pet Vet Guide—Dogs by Martin I. Green. Another great guide to emergency first aid procedures, organized alphabetically by topic. Clear line drawings and concise instructions tell you exactly what you need to know when dealing with a medical crisis.

D: Listings Index

The following list contains the same entries shown in the main directory on pp. 89–245, but this time they are sorted alphabetically by business name—in case you know the name of a particular establishment but aren't sure in exactly which city it is located.

258

269

Super 8 Motel, Corvallis 130
Surf 'n Sand Motel, Newport 186
Surfsand Resort, Cannon Beach 120
Surfside Oceanfront Resort Motel,
    Rockaway Beach 214
Surftides Beach Resort, Lincoln City 172
Sweet Breeze Inn II, Winston 242
Sweet Home Inn, Sweet Home 230
Sweetbrier Inn, Tualatin 236
Table Rock Motel, Bandon 106
Tall Winds Motel, Moro 182
Tasha's Garden–Vacation Rental for People with
    Pets, Cannon Beach 120
Terimore Lodging by the Sea, Netarts 184
Terrace Motel, Coos Bay 128
Thiel Shores Motel, South Beach 226
This Olde House B & B, Coos Bay 128
Three Capes Inn at Netarts, Tillamook 234
Thriftlodge, Grants Pass 150
Thunderhead Lodge Condominiums,
    Government Camp 144
Tiki Lodge Motel, Medford 180
Tiki Lodge Motel, Salem 220
Tilla Bay Motel, Garibaldi 140
Tillamook Inn, Tillamook 234
Tillicum Motor Inn, Umatilla 236
Timbercrest Inn, La Pine 164
TimberLodge Motel, Coos Bay 128
Tolovana Inn, Tolovana Park 234
Tom Tom Motel, Bend 112
Town & Country Motel, Sutherlin 230

E: Topics Index

Yes! — I want to order
Have Dog Will Travel—Oregon Edition

$14.95 for one copy (postage paid)
Buy 2 and save— 2 copies for just $25

Order date _____ Order # _____

Name _____

Address _____

City/state/zip _____

Daytime phone number _____

Send me _____ book(s): $ _____

   Shipping: (any number of books) $ _____ **Free!**

Total order amount: $ _____

Mail this order form with check, money order or credit card information to:

> Ginger & Spike Publications
> PO Box 937
> Wilsonville, OR 97070-0937

In a hurry? For credit card orders:
> **call toll-free 888/255-8030**
> **or fax your order to 503/625-3076**

Credit card no. _____

   Circle one: Visa   MC   exp date _____

Signature _____

Want to travel in **Washington** with your dog? Ask for

Have Dog Will Travel—Washington Edition
Available in mid-1999!

Yes! — I want to order
Have Dog Will Travel—Oregon Edition

$14.95 for one copy (postage paid)
Buy 2 and save— 2 copies for just $25

Order date _____ Order # _____

Name _____

Address _____

City/state/zip _____

Daytime phone number _____

Send me _____ book(s): $ _____

    Shipping: (any number of books) $ _____ **Free!**

Total order amount: $ _____

**Mail this order form with check, money order
or credit card information to:**

    Ginger & Spike Publications
    PO Box 937
    Wilsonville, OR 97070-0937

**In a hurry? For credit card orders:
    call toll-free 888/255-8030
    or fax your order to 503/625-3076**

Credit card no. _____

    Circle one: Visa MC   exp date _____

Signature _____

Want to travel in **<u>Washington</u>** with your dog? Ask for
Have Dog Will Travel—Washington Edition
Available in mid-1999!